2 04

LITURGIES OF THE WILD

LITURGIES
OF THE WILD

Myths That Make Us

MARTIN SHAW

SENTINEL

Sentinel
An imprint of Penguin Random House LLC
1745 Broadway, New York, NY 10019
penguinrandomhouse.com

Grateful acknowledgment is made for permission to reprint lines from "On Raglan Road" by Patrick Kavanagh from *Collected Poems*, edited by Antoinette Quinn (Allen Lane, 2004), reprinted by kind permission of the Trustees of the Estate of the late Katherine B. Kavanagh, through the Jonathan Williams Literary Agency.

Most Sentinel books are available at a discount when purchased in quantity for sales promotions or corporate use. Special editions, which include personalized covers, excerpts, and corporate imprints, can be created when purchased in large quantities. For more information, please call (212) 572-2232 or e-mail specialmarkets@penguinrandomhouse.com. Your local bookstore can also assist with discounted bulk purchases using the Penguin Random House corporate Business-to-Business program. For assistance in locating a participating retailer, e-mail B2B@penguinrandomhouse.com.

Book design by Alissa Rose Theodor

LIBRARY OF CONGRESS CONTROL NUMBER: 2025027258
ISBN 9780593716564 (hardcover)
ISBN 9780593716571 (ebook)

Printed in the United States of America
1st Printing

The authorized representative in the EU for product safety and compliance is Penguin Random House Ireland, Morrison Chambers, 32 Nassau Street, Dublin D02 YH68, Ireland, https://eu-contact.penguin.ie.

For Rob and Sal

CONTENTS

LITURGIES OF THE WILD

Introduction

⸻◦⸻

I felt like I'd never seen a real human being before.

An old man pointed his ceremonial pipe at the rain clouds and started addressing them as if they were dear friends. I can't quite explain why this reduced me to rubble. He spoke gently to the great canopy of sky above us. He wasn't worshipping, but he was certainly negotiating. He was encouraging the clouds to move along. After a few more minutes he turned to me and spoke:

OK, that's enough from me. You actually come from here. Charm them, they're listening.

What followed wasn't promising. At twenty-six my mouth was a prison cell where words went to die. I didn't really know who "they" were. I warbled on self-consciously for a few seconds, then mercifully he picked up the thread and I got retired, absolutely drained from the experience. That night as I tried to sleep I turned the experience around and around in my head. The old man—who had the magnificent name of Wallace Black Elk—was a Lakota Sioux medicine man. You can be sure as an English kid I'd never met one before. Wallace said things that seemed simple but were so raw and fresh they brought tears to my eyes. This wasn't just intelligence, this wasn't just information, this was wisdom.

Why was I even there? I was there because I'd recently sat on a Welsh hillside and fasted for four days and nights. In the bustle of my young life I had stopped. I had walked to a wild place, sat down, and listened. This was something I suspected Wallace would profoundly understand. When he arrived in Britain to teach, mutual friends were able to get me to him. The consequences of the fast had led me to entirely change the life I was previously living as a successful musician. By the time I met the old man, that was all gone, and I had effectively disappeared from polite society entirely. I was out there with the wild things.

Wallace came from a place that seemed half dream to me, the Badlands of South Dakota. Had experienced more hardship, betrayal, and general scuffs than I could in several lifetimes. But he illuminated a world where language mattered, where words could float out of a mouth and make a rowan tree blush, or a blackbird hop onto your hand. It was a sensual, animate earth that sought our attention, especially our praise.

As a young man sarcasm was the commodity I trafficked in. It was what made the experience with the clouds so excruciating; it required sincere, beautiful speech. Who knew if the endeavour worked (author's note: *it did*), but the *attempt*, the sheer chutzpah of it, was devastating.

And I absolutely could not do it.

I travelled with Wallace for two weeks and picked up titbits here and there. He was officially on a lecture tour but loved to dig into his old ceremonial ways as much as possible. You could only keep him at a lectern for a minute or two before he was off in the bush, rummaging around. He endured my questions much as you would a precocious kid. It was clear that all sorts of things that should have arrived in my early life—things of significance—*hadn't*, and he was patiently aware he was talking to an impoverished toddler disguised as a grown human being. I was nothing of the sort. He knew it, I knew it.

I only really viewed Black Elk from a distance, but a quarter of a century ago he seeded a question in me I have tended ever since.

How do you *make* a real human being? And what *is* that?

There's plenty of success in the West. In our post-enlightenment state we've been barrelling along to attempted individuation for several hundred years. The aspiration is the very waters we swim in. It fills our screens, our hand-wringing therapies, our private fantasies. We have more houses, more clothes, more holidays, more prescription drugs than ever before. We live longer and in more luxury than our great grandparents could likely imagine. We have more "stuff" than ever, and yet something often feels missing. What could this mean?

What we lack is the architecture of tempering. There is an adolescent tone to our ambitions, the sheer gimme gimme of them. There's not a lot of real eldership about. We have *stuff*, we know a little about all sorts of things, but would seem oddly weightless to a character like Wallace. Every decade that passes creates young people from many societies who are hypnotised by the same trail of influences; we're losing our bespokeness. We are zip code earth these days. It doesn't have to be like this.

Human beings don't mature just because of breasts, beard, or the like, but by active intervention of what we used to call initiatory encounters, and what, these days, we'd likely call bad luck. Times of travail used to be choreographed into rituals and ceremonies that consciously tempered the human, so when life gave them the squeeze there would be an animal memory as to how to respond, techniques to draw upon.

In the Celtic world you find an old belief. That if you aren't wrapped in the cloak of story and the cloak of place you are liable to experience huge rushes of angst as you age. You are, in some grievous way, unprepared for what the world will likely hurl at you. You remain adolescent, you remain at risk, and that itself makes you dangerous and your decisions likely unwieldy. You're not grown.

When I met Wallace I was a damaged bird, careering around on one wing. I was preeningly self-centered, woefully hurt that the world hadn't recognised my genius—not that I even knew what that could be—and already hardening in my attitude to others. In my early twenties I had a transactional relationship to friendships, and would assess them for their advantageousness. I thought that was what maturity looked like. I pretended ruthlessness was discernment.

I'd left school with no qualifications and quite the chip on my shoulder. Worked in factories, played in bands, skipped from one town to another. "Fly by night" was the phrase. I had a temper and already drank every day—just enough to take the edge off. I had books and records I loved, but creatively I was a jumble, squatting in a magpie's nest of things that glittered mysteriously but often proved to be plastic. My friends seemed less uncertain, bright young things with university and careers ahead of them. I had none of that certainty. It was too early to cast me off as a *complete* failure, but I wasn't far off. I was slipping through the cracks.

Black Elk may have had a lack of fiscal security, but in terms of spiritual wealth he was a rich man. He was immersed in the ritual life of his people from a young age, he had a profound openness and knowledge of the wilds of South Dakota. He had songs in his jaw, he had stories in his soul, he had medicinal knowledge that meant he was loved profoundly. And even as an old man, he would take himself up into the hills with just his blanket and his pipe and talk to all creation as if God was both in everything and standing outside everything. Seems awfully sane to me.

For the first time, I saw a human who seemed profoundly *home*.

He never believed, for a second, he could do anything he wanted in the way we get it drilled into us now. He believed his life—and ours—was to be a master class in site specificity, of listening acutely to what God wanted us to be, and then allowing his circumstances to shape him accordingly. And he was very "show don't tell," Grandpa Wallace. He lived by example. Some First Nations folk hated that he'd be willing to work with white people, but that was his way. If you were with him you'd be praying daily, singing daily, making ceremony frequently, looking out for others, being grateful, and attending, attending, attending to a world in constant disclosure. Wallace was tough, his life was not easy, but he diligently attended to the grace. He believed that anyone doing that—even you and me—could still get made into a real human being, not a hologram, or a brain on legs.

Somehow it never occurred to me that it might be too late for me to become fully human. I somehow presumed that the door of mercy could still—just about—be open to me. At least a crack. I wanted to be like the old man with the pipe. Not to emulate the First Nations, or get caught up in some poverty-rattled New Age imitation, but to seek what *he* sought.

Black Elk encouraged me to live under canvas, to slip away from the wires and lights of modernity, to tune up my aboriginal ear to locate the wider news of the universe. In his own way he advised me to dive into what is sometimes called "the matter of Britain," the myths and landscape of this strange North Atlantic island. To become a custodian of its stories, to learn to decipher its hedgerow gossip.

For me, that involved leaving behind a great deal of what I thought I valued. A career as a musician, the tail end of a marriage, a Tourette's-like syndrome of sarcastic tics and droll asides that ensured whatever feeble status I had in my peer group.

Without a phone in my pocket or a laptop in my bag I went looking for whatever wild pockets of England I could still find. I spent
four years in a tent, and by the time I emerged there was a kind of
roughage to my ideas and a little soul to my words that simply could
not come any other way. I became a praise maker. I apprenticed to
two things: place and story.

Over those years I trained as a wilderness rites-of-passage guide.
The process focuses on a four-day and -night fast completely alone in
a wild place. During that time you are disrobed of many of life's distractions, the experience often being a complete revelation. The earth
rushes towards you, and surprisingly without hurt feelings. Traditionally the process is usually first experienced at the hinge between
adolescence and young adulthood, but can be revisited at many of
life's crossroads. It clears the decks both spiritually and psychologi-
cally, opening up our questions to a receptive universe. In Snowdonia
in Wales I worked with at-risk youth, the dying, the troubled, the
curious over that period. It was exacting and tremendously healing.
Healing in the way it gave me a sense of both vocation and place:
Through long sits in the wild I no longer felt like a tourist on this
earth, someone just passing through. I had invested in a small, specific
region and was determined to court its many layers of disclosure.

I completely submersed myself in the myths and stories of my
culture. They would become my wayward aunts and fearsome uncles:
The scrapes and challenges in these tales helped my psyche begin
to form a more substantial shape. I grew less afraid of depth. I began
to trust myself. I saw that kindness mattered. In my way, I began the
process of becoming someone I could bear to glimpse in the mirror.

A myth is a story that speaks of our relationship to the gods, the
earth, the animals, the elements, fellow humans. They orientate. They
are the soil that children-as-plants are meant to be grown in. If the

soil isn't rich enough the kid grows wonky. The roots of this child are not meant to hit the limits of a plastic bucket but extend out into a decent acreage of wilderness.

Myths should mature you. *Mature* is a word that doesn't excite us much, but it should. We should cleave to it, puzzle over it, wonder at it. Maturity, however, is not always what the gods display. The gods in mythology often amplify the panorama of human ambition, from sacrifice to betrayal to glory and beyond. They are often comedic, terrifying, and worst of all, eternal. To live forever means you don't really possess pathos. Weight, soul, heft comes from the yoke of our finiteness, our puzzled humanity in the face of our consciousness.

The maturity many myths engender is by showing us—writ large—the passions that roar through our body and we attempt to understand. Those passions have names. When we feel lust or love or fright we are maybe in the presence of Aphrodite, Aengus Óg, or Loki. We become wiser by having these often-underground presences afforded the names our ancestors were given for them. Rather than being ragdolled by their impulses we learn how to libate them, subdue them, or invoke them at the right times. This is an ancient technology that enables emotional literacy. However, no one in ancient Greece would point to their chest and indicate that this was all happening inside them and nowhere else. That would be mad. No, the gods were also out *there* in stuff: trees, goats, mountains, a cup of wine, or a feather that floated up between a woman's legs and made a baby.

As they grow us, myths tell us about the conditions of life, what to expect, what it looks like.

Today, I'm a storyteller. In the language of my Celtic ancestors, that would make me a seanchaí. This is not the type that turns up at reenactment fairs or kids' parties. I don't have a harp or cloak. And I don't just tell any kind of tale; I tell stories that have many secrets in them: old codes for a new world. These myths are rarely cosy experiences; they are less to do with enchantment and far more with waking up. The stories I tell can last days, up to five when I've really got the bit between my teeth. I've told such tales in lecture halls to hundreds or round fires to a dozen, sometimes with snowflakes nesting in my beard.

I've taught courses at Stanford University, lectured at Oxford and Cambridge, and have written eighteen books on the subject of myth and its meanings. My own school of independent scholars is twenty-two years old, its first home a black tent I lived in. My original students numbered three and are now on average seventy a year, coming to study with me on the Celtic fringe of the British Isles. I've created several postgraduate master's programmes and was Reader in Poetics at Dartington Hall for several years.

I love what I get to do. This is not just a world of Newtonian logic and spreadsheets. I walk out of a longhouse after a night of storytelling and I meet an old Miwok man keeping guard in the grasses with a stick. He tells me the stories I tell may attract snakes. A Tibetan storyteller finishes a night of telling and is paid the highest of all compliments. A bowl of sand is brought to their feet by their audience. The teller is told the people are waiting for horses' hooves to appear in that sand, so vivid was the telling, so true was the incantation.

What I do is help people find their way into the rigour and delight of relationship to story and place. These stories can range from the roving grandeur of *The Odyssey* to an issue in their love or work life. I work a kind of yoga of the imagination, stretching the connections between the grand old epics and the intimacy of our own life's challenges. It coaxes consciousness to do this, raises delight, and to some it feels like coming home.

When this is absent, we're going to take facsimiles over nothing at all. We will create stories that simply support the narrative of endless, exponential growth rather than the cautions and limits that have always supported traditional mythologies. We will settle for myth-lite. Myths that challenge nothing, and engage only in a rather tedious celebration of ourselves and only ourselves.

Many of us are driven by stories we barely understand and rarely investigate. Family narratives that reared into life long before we were born can prove to be the mandate we dreamily hitch our wagon to. The more unexamined, the more corrosive, even dangerous they can become. And stories matter. Cultures get built on them. This is a book that rescues lost stories. Many come from the fairy-tale and mythic traditions of the world, relegated these last hundred years to children's books or a therapist's couch. As a professor and writer of many books on myth, I say this is tremendous folly, and that we are wandering initiatory times but lacking an initiatory language. An initiation is something that instructs us, and often in the form of a crisis.

I've told you a little about Wallace, and the profundity of meeting him. But the most radical thing he ever had to tell me came at our very last moment together. It was something so unexpected I buried it for almost twenty-five years.

We were deep in a sweat lodge. It's very hot—imagine the most roasting sauna you've ever experienced—and completely black save the glow of hot rocks in a pit. Wallace is a sun-dancer, so this is what's known as a warrior sweat. Proper, slam dunk, visionary heat. For a moment the prayers are gently rested, and the door flap is opened. Life-reviving air enters.

In the slant of moonlight coming from the door flap I can briefly see the old man. There is a sheen of sweat on his face, his long plaits resting on his chest. He seems to be looking at something the rest of us can't see. After a time he briefly gestures to the shape of the sweat lodge. *The sweat lodge is like a skinboat. Ancient kind of boat, made out of hide. It will carry you from one place to another. You will not be who you were when you began the journey. You arrive at another shore. Sacred place. And your body too, another skinboat you grow into when you become a real human being. Takes a whole life. You have to know a lot of stories.*

I suddenly feel like I'm in church and this is the sermon I've waited my whole life to hear.

As if he knows what I'm thinking, Wallace turns to me in the dark and whispers: *The little hippie guy. Jesus. We knew he was coming. We'd heard his words. Long before white folks told us. He was in Turtle Island too. Don't give up on him now, he hasn't given up on you.*

This is not what you expect to hear from a shaman. This is the last thing I would have wanted to hear. Having abandoned Christianity with full vigour at seventeen, coming from a house of preachers and signs and wonders, well, this was a wonder too much. I didn't want to see the slim finger of the medicine man pointing to what I'd been running from. He was pointing towards the faith of my earliest days. I couldn't imagine anything less sexy.

If we follow where Black Elk's finger is pointing this is what we find.

I sit in the pew of Upton Vale Baptist Church, and I drift in and out of consciousness. I am about ten. As usual I notice things that don't seem directly to do with the service. The way the light drifts slantwise through the stained glass windows, the delicate particles of dust it illuminates, the grain of the wood I am sitting on. I wonder if God lives in these things as much as the sermon that is trundling by. Does God live everywhere, speak to us everywhere, or only in the

Bible? Could I feel him talking to me in birdsong, or the roar of the sea, even a dream? Is that even *allowed*, that kind of free-range Christianity? It doesn't seem clear.

Later I shake the preacher's big hand as I leave the church and I walk home with Dad. Sometimes we walk up through the woods behind the house we live in. I much prefer the woods to church. I love how sweet and pungent the air is, I love the shady places, and most of all what it seems to do to my dad's imagination. Banished are the easy-to-read, three-step allegorical illustrations of church and suddenly I'm hearing about centaurs and naiads, of Robin and Marian, of Arthur of the Britons, of Merlin and Morgan le Fay. I mean, c'mon. *This* is the news.

To my imaginative taste buds we've gone from skimmed milk to a dram of Ardbeg whisky. I'm dizzy. As Dad talks and walks—his hands shaping scenes in the air—I run alongside, the hairs on my neck standing up. This is the stuff. This is where my deep heart dwells.

I associate church entirely with hymns and sermons. The sermons speak good sense (and are probably terrific for the old folks) but there doesn't seem to be much contemplative spaciousness. Worst of all, there seems to be no urgency. How are you going to keep a young man with an ounce of heart in your church without a little urgency, a sense of vocation even? I don't hear about wild old hermits and visionaries and dreamers, or if I do, they are from thousands of years ago, safe within the nailed-down pages of the Good Book. But I don't want the pages nailed down. Cormorants should be sweeping in and out of those pages, otters nesting, trees growing. But we are always indoors, and *our religion seems indoors too.*

Wallace, against what I could ever have expected, was gesturing to Christianity as a liturgy of the wild. A kind of communion that wasn't meant to be restricted to a stone building with a few dozen people, but issuing out in all directions. Up with the magpie in her nest, down with the adder in the Somerset grasses. All God's creations. In his few words I glimpsed—uncomfortably—a wider, more alive, more embracing sense of the God of my childhood than I'd ever entertained.

I would spend years living in the tent locating what I couldn't find in Christianity. For an awfully long time this search paid enormous rewards. It still does. I forgot about Wallace's words, content with my wild stories that remained outside the ken of the religion of my childhood. But when I approached my fiftieth birthday that was all about to change, though I had no inkling.

I decided that I was going to extend my experience of wilderness vigils, break out into new ground again, intensify the human instinct to lean into wisdom.

This is what I made my mind up to do.

For 101 days I would walk into a Dartmoor forest and tell it a story. I called these offerings *Calling Songs*. What I was calling to I didn't quite know. After the telling I would sit, often at dusk, and just listen to the wood. I can slip into that kind of frequency easily because of my many years of following such a practice. The 101 days was taxing, repetitive, sometimes marvellous. I learnt an awful lot about fidelity, of simply showing up, again and again.

Come one very chill January evening I had finally come to the end of this ritual. The last night was a journey to the very centre of the forest, to an Iron Age hill fort, where I would sit up all night in prayer. Picture the scene: With a full belly and mug of tea drunk, I set out from my cottage up the path into the trees. The ground was frosty and everything seemed to glitter. I was aware of the occasional distant stag bellow as I thumped up the frozen rutted track with just a wee bit of moonlight coming down through the oaks. I could hear the urgent rush of the Dart River down the hill to my left and I felt some jubilance that this would all soon be over. It had been a heady and disorientating few months. But now I felt grounded and solid within myself. The night vigil was more a formality really, a sign-off, a doing-things-proper at the end of a long act of service. I wasn't expecting anything from it.

The first few hours passed uneventfully, the high blue cry of the occasional owl somewhere to the right above my head. I remember being aware there would be the bones of the long dead down somewhere in the frozen mud of the hill fort. Somewhere in the third watch of the night I remembered what I'd brought with me. Two rocks I'd fished out of the Dart earlier that day. When I'd brought them home, I'd realised they were actually one rock that had split. Who knows how many years they had resided under the brown-green waters of that freezing river? So near each other but apart.

I decided to stand, and to knock the stones together.

Clack clack clack.

I made a very simple prayer of thanks, for the many blessings and disciplines learnt from the 101 days, and openness on this last night for any last insights.

Creator, what would you have me do?

For a minute or two nothing happened. I looked around—as I'm liable to do—the dim shapes of trees and holly bushes. Nowt. Nada. Business as usual. I felt relief almost.

Then I did something I never do. I looked up. Past the trees into the sky. And it was then that I saw it.

It was a light rapidly falling to earth, the colours being similar to the aurora borealis—the northern lights. And when I say falling to earth I mean aimed directly at me. This all took place over a few seconds. My jaw dropped and is still dropped. I saw it change shape, so it became like an arrowhead moving at breathtaking, impossible speed. What I was seeing seemed an entry into the marvellous. As a wilderness rites-of-passage guide of twenty-five years I've seen some things, but nothing like that. It was painfully beautiful, seemingly impossible. An arrow falling from the sky. I just couldn't move. If this was the end, then it was a pretty bloody amazing way to go.

At the last moment—and this is an event that is both only a few seconds long but continually unfolding to me to this day—the arrow plunged directly into the trees just a few feet to my right. Utterly silent, these luminescent greens and pale whites seemed to be just sucked into the pitch dark of the pungent forest floor and disappear.

I sat up for the rest of the night, agape, ecstatic. I wasn't frightened. I even danced.

Around dawn I staggered back down the frost-glittered track set out before me. I was bushed, amazed, sore, emotional. I sat at my kitchen table and gripped the sturdy weight of the timber. I looked in the mirror and patted my own head incredulously. As if checking I was still alive.

But it wasn't over. Not quite.

As I finally clambered into bed, I closed my eyes and saw nine words: *Inhabit the Time and Genesis of Your Original Home.*

I really didn't understand what that could mean, not in my thoughts at least. My body may have. It's an odd phrase; with little skips that make it hard to pin down, it flips like a salmon in the hand and is gone. Such words require a kind of devotional chewing to gradually glean the protein. I knew from my family line that the understanding was that our original home was—dare I even think it, let alone say it—*Eden.* I had not thought about that word for a long, long time.

So I go out into the bush for 101 days, peer into the mysteries as deeply as I possibly can, and I find the mossy face of *Christ* staring back at me? This just can't be happening.

The two sides of that rock so long separated had found themselves again.

And later the dreams came.

One night I dreamt of a figure of light who simply brought me into itself for possibly twenty seconds. The love that emanated from this embrace was barely quantifiable in human terms. It was devastating; it doesn't exist as far as I can tell in the usual human range of sense experience. It was every hug, every much-needed weep, every longed-for reunion happening all at once. It was high tide in the heart. Everything I'd ever loved was in this holding, and a whole lot more this bear of little brain had never experienced. I panicked, and immediately the intensity dropped to a slightly more manageable level. It somehow communicated to me without using words. It said that every act of loving care between people on the planet (and animals, funnily enough) had, secreted within it, an echo of this original, enormous love it had for all of us. Our little moments of intimacy and affection were all spiderwebbed up to this being.

It also told me that I should watch the sun rise as often as I could. That there was something in the act of dawn that would be good for me to keep witnessing. Since then I've slept in a room facing east, and I keep the curtains open. I will never, ever forget this dream.

One night I dreamt I was in a war in a faraway land. I was in a ditch with my captain, the ground around us dismal and dark. He gestured to my left arm. I hadn't noticed how oddly shaped it was. He said I had been through a great battle and had done my very best through trial and error to fix my arm. It just about functioned but was pretty mangled. As he said it, it was as if I was suddenly seeing my arm through his eyes. I didn't know I had been dragging it around like that. I couldn't see his face exactly, but he said to me that, if I wanted, he could heal my arm. But to fix it, he would have to break it first. I was suddenly frightened, terrifically vulnerable. As if all of me was visible to this man. But I took a breath and agreed. And if it hurt, it only hurt for a second.

One night I dreamt I was on a ship. But the ship was somewhere out in the marvellous, somewhere out in the darkness of the heavens. There was the captain again, again I couldn't quite see his face. He was steering the vessel with this great wheel. He said the wheel, which was behind everything I could see, had three points on it that he constantly and subtly moved between. The wheel was never still, he said, but dynamic. And the secret of the wheel was as much the movement between the three points as the points themselves. He told me everything I could imagine had this moving wheel within it, no matter how terrifically small.

One night I dreamt I was in St. Colman's cave in Ireland. Suddenly a stag appeared at the entrance to the cave, illuminated by moonlight. As I gazed at the majestic animal I realised I was terrifically thirsty. It leaned forward and I realised it had drops of water on the tip of every antler.

I put my hands together and held them out. The primordial beast leant his head forward and I caught the drops. Drops that quenched a thirst much more profound than a dry mouth.

One night I dreamt I was walking, and as I walked I passed many people. Moving through and around these folks were Elohim, spirits of the air, both positive and negative in character. These beings were visible and advising us. No one was independent of these constantly arising encounters. It was what humans did with these persuasions and influences that mattered. I called to the captain and asked him why couldn't we see these spiritual energies in our waking lives? It would make everything so much simpler. All of humanity would then see this reality, acknowledge it, and we would know in a much clearer way what we were all battling.

But what would be the use of faith? a voice said. *You would not grow in the way I wish if that reality was made visible to you.*

Some say that dreams are a personal mythology, and mythology is a community dream. These weren't that. They were sensorially outside my life's experience of dreaming. They came from someplace else. But that brings me round to myth. There's very little in the world that tells me more about the experience of life than mythology. I have absolutely devoted myself to it for twenty-five years. It is a gift that keeps on giving. Much of it is luminous with wisdom. For anyone wishing to understand their own impulses on a grand scale I recommend the old stories. To understand how we have spoken across species using story I recommend the old stories. Go to the Greek, the Aboriginal, the Irish, the Siberian. They tell us so very much about life. They are tattooed onto me. They show us the great fundament of the lived experience.

Myths told me all about life, but this myth, this Yeshua, crashing like that January arrow into human time, told me how to *live* that life. For me, that directive resides most radically in that most punk rock of teachings, the Beatitudes. I found my final and greatest teacher. I became a Christian. Or, more likely, I realised I *was* a Christian. Just not a very good one. A little out of focus.

As Yeats put it, Christ's "uncontrollable mystery" had arrived.[1] In the Irish of my ancestors, Creator had come like a *Ropadh*—a blast of the wind—with Christ as the *Seabhac Gaoithe*—the wind hawk—and all my smirking ideas were *Greamanna Seabhaic A Dhéanamh De Rud*—torn to bits by hawk bites. Now I was hungry. Hungry for a

Christianity as huge as the forest, as magnificent as the stars that swirled overhead, as endless as the River Dart I heard rushing past. Have at me Lord of the Elements, I submit.

I was baptised in late winter, in the depths of a Dartmoor river, by a man as much goat as priest. My father beside me, us all slip and slidy and jubilant into the dark currents. Afterwards I sat on the bank and wept like a child.

Now I had to find a church.

It's a tiny ancient church that found *me* in the end. Completely surrounded by shops. Saint Pancras of Rome it's called, in the city of Exeter in rural England. Surrounding this Anglo-Saxon structure is a perfumery, multiple food stalls, a newsagent selling porn and fizzy drinks, shouting kids, and many cafés. It's Sunday but it could be any day of the week. It's a chaotic scene, and I'm wandering around wondering if this can really, really be the place. I mean, *c'mon*. This is not a promising start.

First thing I detect is a scent. Incense, Byzantine incense.

Through the reek of frying onions and burgers I catch this heartstopping, otherworldly scent. It's coming from a small doorway cut into ancient red Devon stone. I follow the scent, enter the Orthodox service, and absolutely everything changes. I mean like day to night changes.

For two hours I enter a kind of Christian Dreaming that is so deep it is without beginning or end. Every ten minutes it seems another door to another century—both before my life and after it— is opening. I am in a *participation mystique*. Finally, the deep interior in me is getting fed, and I'm not thinking about myself one little bit.

When it's over I am unable to move. After fifty years of heading for the door the second a service is finished, I'm absolutely stock-still. Near tears. Most of what has happened I don't understand, not intellectually. But my soul has set out on divine waters. Almost none of the modern tick lists for spirituality were supplied: no checking in with the attendees, no slide projector and uplifting gospel worship, no turning to your neighbour and saying hello. The Orthodox priest rarely seems to look much in our direction at all.

But something is happening. On the exterior what we witness is the repetition of very old words, swinging bowls of incense, the occasional kissing of an icon. But this is just the outside. For this absolute beginner the presence of the Galilee Druid has announced himself. For this absolute beginner a door has opened to nighttime starry deserts and burning bushes and a fish with coins in its mouth. Like babushka dolls, as the liturgy progresses, older and older images push forward, one inside the other. There seems to be a trackway here back to the very beginning of Christianity.

When it comes time for the Eucharist—communion—I find myself compelled to take it. There seems to be no choice in the matter. I watch my body walk me up to the priest without delay. I've been waiting fifty years, I can't wait any longer. It was a little hasty, and rather against protocol, but it just sort of happened.

I have plans for the rest of the afternoon but have to cancel them. I drive through a red light on the way home, shouting to hooting drivers that *I've been to church and have no idea what is happening!* I lie in my darkened bedroom and let all I've described to you move through me. I feel different, and the feeling doesn't pass. It was like wildness and discipline dancing with each other.

For the next year I attend the church. The priest doesn't hound me to join—quite the opposite. He doesn't slap a flyer in my hand or waggle the collection box. He explains almost nothing. He just says, *If you like it, why not come back? See if it sticks.* I'm used to the hard sell, not this spacious approach. But it's in keeping with Orthodoxy. *We've been around since AD 33, we don't do things in a hurry.* It's all new to me; the sermons being only five minutes in length, the sung theology of the service, the *dance* of the Divine Liturgy, the sheer physicality of it all: kissing icons, crossing oneself, prostrations, fasting for the hours beforehand, adjusting to standing up for long periods. It's very slow, but it is a kind of dance. Later on the Sunday, I always value the slight ache in my legs as I finally sit down to break bread. No one shoved a doughnut in my face or broke down into bullet points quite what was going on. Because what is going on is a profound mystery. It is doing its work on me. Is it easy? No, not really. It's substantial and requires attention.

From the outside, Orthodoxy has seven particular scars across its hide: the seizing of Antioch, Alexandria, and Jerusalem by the Muslims; the two sackings of Constantinople; the burning of Kiev by the Mongols; and most recently the Russian Revolution (*not even getting into the Great Schism*). Yet the resilience of Orthodoxy has never been profoundly compromised. It was a little of that antiquity that I encountered that day I entered the liturgy. And yet, how could something so very old seem so incredibly fresh? It was like a glimpse of Eden, or even heaven.

Orthodoxy—the clue may seem to be in the name—can sometimes be regarded as a rather repetitive and dogmatic business. But that's not how we either understand or experience it. The Tradition *is* the Life, and within the Life is a ferment of creativity. It's a tradition with regeneration as well as conservation; Orthodoxy's connection to the Holy Spirit was not neatly wrapped up in the early centuries. There's fresh bread being baked, make no mistake. As John says,

"When the spirit of truth has come, He will guide you into all truth."[2] As I keep attending, I simply can't believe the providence of what's happened.

Every Thursday I speak to Father for about an hour. The conversation goes where it will. A lot of the time we're laughing, or silent, or I'm pushing some enquiry or another. After a few months he offers some advice: *Stop reading for a bit. Orthodoxy is first for the body not the intellect. That'll come quite naturally. Stay focused on the Encounter, not the theology. Stay focused on the Presence not the history. There's nothing wrong with study, but don't rush there too quickly.* As the time comes for reception I struggle. It's a tough period and suddenly the intimacy of the dreams and the encounters with grace are far away. As all Christians know, this is where the rubber hits the road. Feeling ecstatic and groovy is one thing, but there has to be more going on than that. There has to be discipline. There has to be a praxis you return to that is not dependent on being spiritually high to undergo it. In the last six weeks I begin to discover quite what that looks like.

In the last few days I experience something that is rather akin to an exorcism. Father breathes over me, then delivers a series of very old prayers, prayers that would aggravate anything unsavoury lingering in the recesses of my character. It's like getting a spiritual MRI scan. I renounce the Devil and accept God. I'm walked to the door of the church and actually spit at the Adversary. I am barefoot. I remain relatively sanguine throughout, and I notice there's a kind of peacefulness in me for the week afterwards. It did something; it was by no means an empty ceremony. I realise that I'll feel the benefit of such a thing every few months to be quite honest.

The day comes for reception. Some family and friends are gathered in this beautiful old Anglo-Saxon church I've come to regard as home. I remove my shoes and socks and read the Creed. Old words are said by Father, words that are a high bar in beauty and almost intimidating in what is required of me. These are words to wreath a warrior, not just a hermit. They have pluck and fire in them. It's like something being carved on a breastplate. There's a sense of being swathed protectively in the words, even as we go out to meet the world.

Finally I am given a name: *Petroc.*

Petroc was an old Celtic saint who was said to travel with a wolf. He did much ministering in the lands I was born in. He said *yes* to the universe. Such a name makes you sit up a little straighter, makes you a little stronger in your resolve. It is a name to earn. Those early saints, they often gave their liturgies in the wild places. It just lands different out there, out where the buses don't park.

What kind of book have you opened? A book with two intentions: Firstly, to provide you with mythologies that are expert in ushering people through life's travails, that do in fact speak in an initiatory tone, that provide a seam of ideas and images to gird your way in troubling times. Something you can hang your heart on. Secondly, to show you that by nesting in these great myths you in turn start to sift the subterranean narratives of your own life to consciousness. If your story is a river, then myth is the ocean it should naturally lead to.

Each chapter circles a theme in the panoramic development of getting grown. From passivity to limit, from dream to vision, we encounter stories and ideas to assist the experience of really being a human. I have chosen themes that, though sometimes distinctly unglamorous, are universal in experience. Another writer may present them in a painstakingly particular progression, but I think life is more chaotic than that. Loss, desire, opportunity—they fall upon us at different times, they are site specific to our lives. So one chapter may have more resonance than another, but circle back in five years and it may be a different theme entirely that speaks to you.

This is a book in which we begin to regather our lost stories. We gather them this way: We become conscious of how the great themes of myth speak through our own years. When this happens, our own stories gain a shape and purpose we may never have dreamed of. This is a book about how to get home. Home in our bones, our wonder, our eccentricity, our steadfastness. Home in our curves, wrinkles, opinions, and griefs. The sheer, humble nobility of being lucky enough to be born at all. There are many of us with second houses and pensions who are nowhere near anything that feels like home.

It's subtle what I'm suggesting. It will require work. It will be through discernment rather than bullet points that these connections get strengthened. But having worked with thousands of people, from Stanford University to a Minnesotan longhouse, it's not an idle promise. Humans are made of stories, and so we should be seeking the ones that call forth the best in us. This often provokes a longer road and a greater cost; it involves a covenant with limit. But without these stories testing and deepening us, we remain as children, even as the house burns.

My hope is there will be something hauntingly familiar in what we explore. Like an Irish fiddle heard in a busy street, or a heron taking wing over a Dorset river. Something with a rather lovely ache to it. Encountering the Ancient Good feels more like this than something disorientatingly hip, a shrill newness for the sake of being new. That kind of thing doesn't tend to stand the test of time. Myth does. That's why it deserves to be called a myth.

And who or what is the Ancient Good? It is the deepest encounter that could be found in these pages. It is the call to conscience, it is the push to truth, it is the holiness of night and the sheer vivacity of dawn. It is what stands behind all these things. It is the best of what is in all these things.

This weave of folktales, biblical stories, and personal accounts is an attempt to prompt your soul into communication. To initiate you into knowing deep down that this world is mysterious yet approachable, and that a story well-loved can hold both the everyday and the supremely luminous in its hand. The sensation of those two in relationship can create—without any conscious pressure at all—an awareness of profound meaning. And from meaning comes purpose and from purpose comes a sharpening to the sheer privilege of living at all. It's in this combination that the myths make us.

ON THROWN
AWAY STORIES

I ask him for a dream and the veteran's distressed. High colour, heavyset, hands tapping knees, a light sheen of sweat, he'd rather be anywhere but here. But he has no distance left to run. The diets don't work, the therapy doesn't work, even the Bible isn't working. Nothing will work because Jeff has a secret. A story. Unsaid words that have been eating him up from the inside for almost fifty years. There was a war in the East that Jeff never came back from. But today, finally, the story's going to get told. The whole sprawling extraordinary mess of it. In a hut in the backwoods of Minnesota a taboo will get broken. Jeff will say the thing he cannot say. I tell the small group of veterans that we won't be stopping for supper until the story's over. Late summer light slants through the window and lands in the circle between us, dust suddenly visible.

Ruth is sitting with her back against a rowan tree in a Dartmoor forest. She's talking about the rape she endured at fourteen as if it happened to someone else. The horror's been told so often it's taken on a literary polish. I listen and prod the fire. I then ask her to tell the story in a way she's never done before. Not for the podcast listeners or TED Talk. Not as a motivational speech about overcoming adversity. No, tell it like a fairy tale. Tell it in the third person. Something unexpected happens when you do that. Something beyond your own imaginative choreography. She tells the story in this way: *Once upon a time, at the end of her childhood, a young woman found herself lost in the forest.* Suddenly tears fall like rain. She stays with it, gasping and occasionally silenced but valiantly holding the thread. And, at the end, I ask her the old story-time question: *And what happened next?* Suddenly the earth is ancient and listening closely to her.

I'm driving Gary back to his house on a Plymouth council estate. He's off drugs, off servicing men behind the bus station, out of the gang his brother runs. But only *just,* these things being a magnet he keeps floating towards. Sometimes he wants to talk to me about his life, sometimes not, and the change can be in a fraction of a second. Last time we did he threatened to hurl himself into the fast-moving current of a river we were passing. But today's different, today he wants a story. I tell him a tale about a girl leaving a village for good, and not one pair of eyes is on her wishing her well. At this he moans for a bit, rocks a bit, then makes a grab for the gear stick, tries to uproot it from the stem and bring the car off the road. I pull over and he starts pummelling his own head. *Get it out of my head,* he says. *Get the story away from me, it's in me, I don't like it, what have you done?* This from a young man who watches horror, porn, and plays war games on an almost hourly rotation. A tiny folk tale has unearthed something in its terrible simplicity that's gone straight to his heart. *That's me, the girl is me, no one, no one, is looking out for me.* I hug him for a moment and tell him, *I am.* To get to you, they have to come through me. Whoever they may be. He cries then opens the car door.

It's January, and it's dark. A great blast of freezing air gallops into the car. For a moment he's lit up under a streetlamp before darting into the shadows. I will never see him again.

There's no one in this whole wide world that isn't carrying a story. You could be president, a yoga teacher, a junkie, and you have this one completely unique thing in your pocket. Your story. It may be crumpled like a bus ticket or writ large on tablets of stone, but it's yours. And God almighty you need to tell it, to rest in it, to find some peace with it. You may realise this at twenty or ninety, but one day you'll realise it.

As we age life moves fast. It seems to speed up, and sometimes any kind of coherent narrative seems lost in the crosswinds. But every now and then, there will be a moment of coincidence or even providence that makes us stop and scratch our head. We catch a glimpse of meaning. And then we are distracted, look away, and focus on something shiny and exotic. But in that distraction can be a discarding of something that is absolutely ours, distinct and site-specific. That's the real gold, the little crumbs of plum cake leading us home when we are lost in the wires and lights of a world growing at a mechanized not human pace. The treasure is when you locate something that feels properly, authentically yours. Its treasure is its specificity not its universality.

The question is: Why do we throw our stories away? Why do we undervalue them? I think it's to do with attention. We are perennially distracted. In the past it would have been the sheer heft of raising a family, earning a living, the struggle and gain of our years. That alone was absorbing enough, and all are noble attentions. And we had myths that made them so, that mirrored such attentions back to us, but with dignified, spiritual dimensions. These days social media pulls us in a variety of directions, but the general emphasis being achievement and visibility. In comparison to Hollywood or even Tik-Tok ideals, our own strange walk may seem unexceptional. It's easier to just focus on something more glamourous. It seems that there's quite the divide between the happy face we post online and the disinterest we actually have in the narrative of our own years.

The first step is to take a breath and dare to entertain the thought that in the debris of your life would be stories worth examining. That they are, as I just wrote, a kind of treasure.

The less we do this, the more unanchored we become, and susceptible to a virtual reality that will fill our entire waking hours given a ghost of a chance. To give your lost stories some attention is a surprisingly radical act.

As a teenager I had a friend, Johnny, who lived nearby. There wasn't much money in his house or mine. But mine did have heating. His mum had split, dad was day drinking. Johnny would come up to our place in midwinter just to lean against the radiator before trudging home. His bedroom had a spare mattress where his father's drinking pals would collapse at the end of a night's boozing. It could be a shadowy world at times, the kind of place you may not want to think about again if you got out.

But he did something unusual. Johnny took the conditions of his upbringing seriously. He took them mythically. They were not random. He combed through fairy tales, stories of Cronos devouring his children. He made a home for the testing conditions of early years. He storied it. He afforded his life the dignity of serious attention. He started to write poems. He learnt a musical instrument, started to dance. His introduction to dark experience he turned to his advantage. He had empathy and a certain sobriety in understanding people's inner motivations. He had Underworld knowledge. Many of the kids in his science class were innocents in comparison. He didn't go looking for disorder, but he'd found a primeval device to grow corn from ashes. He'd found myth.

It wasn't glamourous, Johnny's growing. He could have easily crushed it under his heel and created another persona. He didn't do that. He gathered his tales in, gave them form, and in doing so they did not unconsciously run the show. When he spoke of his story, it had the protein of a fairy tale, and when he told a fairy tale it had the grit of lived experience. He threaded them together. Thirty years on, with children and a PhD, he lives a very different story. But even so, Johnny ennobles those early experiences a place at the table.

As we think about stories, I'd suggest two things are happening these days. On the one hand we have more public confessions than ever—chat show, podcast variety—and at the very same moment we are drowning in a deficit of deeper meaning, deeper communication. Our addiction to the cult of *I* and the social mediums to communicate that *I* is no replacement for profound, dare I say it, soulful disclosure. According to ancient sources the soul is not impressed by much we hurl at it. It discriminates, usefully.

I knew a woman who'd always been rich. Lived on a big pot of family money; it was never, ever going to run out. Julia's story was one of the best education, holidays that took months not weeks, and courting various movers and shakers, even a Scandinavian prince. But when she spoke of it her voice took on a flat, even embarrassed, tone. Julia's story didn't have the drama of a story like Johnny's, and she was keen to throw it away. She had become expert at conceal-ment. But the only job in town that's truly ours is to be conscious of our own story. When you can speak of it honestly, it can become useful to others. If it remains co-opted by shame, others sense it and we become hard to trust.

One day we took a walk through a wood. As we strolled I told her the story of Parzival riding through the wasteland of ancient Britain. On the outside he was resplendent and privileged, on the inside he was filled with doubt and confusion. "The slum must be inside us," as the poets say. Julia slowly grew to resituate her experience. It too had something to say. Endless privilege can be a monster all its own. Damaging to soul, wonder, and a sense of vocation. Gradually she started to locate the adversarial encounters and sudden marvels of her own years hidden up in the castle's tower. Like Rapunzel, the stories became threads she could lower to the ground, and all sorts of rich and earned experiences could climb up to meet her. There is no one-size-fits-all to a mythic life. Her mythologies were different to Johnny's, seemingly subtler, but no less tricky.

People say I must be thrilled by modern life because it's called the Hermian Age. You may remember Hermes is the Greek god of the storytellers and instant communication between people. Surely this is what's happening now? Ah, friends, draw closer. We're not address-ing the fine print in Hermes's contract. His connection is only suc-cessful *soul to soul.* If the soul is not roused, Hermes is simply not present. We are living in a facsimile of that rapidity; our ears are filled with story but maybe not myth. I will come to the difference soon.

Tristan and Isolde is still playing itself out in fraught love affairs all across America, *Beowulf* is called forth in the sheer guts of trying to piece yourself together after a rough divorce. It's my job, my civic duty, my privilege to track the myth hanging onto the wingtip of the personal anecdote, or the tale you are trying to brush aside. The myth is moved from confessional to majestic, from persona to pres-ence. It's always a mistake to tell a myth exactly what it is: They contract from sight, stop delivering protein when we do that. We are left with an allegory, not a mystery, and that's no kind of trade. We are suddenly standing with a pelt, not a wild animal.

Myths are wily enough to remember they have a connection to the oral tradition. Something preliterate. In a promiscuous way they have moved from mouth to mouth, settlement to settlement over the centuries. Their particular power is that they refer to what I call both the *timebound* and the *timeless*. The gritty complexity of life but also the miraculous that surrounds us if we dare but behold it. Mythic awareness is always moving us from seeing to *beholding* life, in its multidimensional, irrational, providential, tragic, and glorious dimensions. It is the royal road to the deepest depths of the psyche.

What is your own creation story? What characters and events helped form you? There will be fairy tales brushing up to all sorts of experiences we disregard. Myths assist in the growing of consciousness and the slow tempering of maturity. They are not just patterns or codes, they are allies.

When we reach for a myth to help recover our own stories, we make connections with the little *I* and the big *We*, and in doing so, shrug off a little unnecessary loneliness. In place of isolation we now have the camaraderie of being worked within a bigger story.

This is no small thing we're doing, anchoring ourselves to the most extraordinary source of wisdom. Myths are north stars to a culture deserving of the name, culture coming from the Latin, *colere*, which means to till the ground. To make a culture you dig down into a story. That story needs to be robust enough to explain a few things whilst also accommodating mystery. Myths hold together heaven and earth, they are a crossroads between the timeless and the timebound. Myths are connecting tissue between us and the universe.

Myths can be the words that underpin a ritual, or actually are a ritual themselves. They often explicate our origins, the gods, the visible and invisible worlds. They have images so emphatic and nourishing that humans can organise their philosophies around them. They afford dignity and purpose to the highly reactive experience of living. They intrigue us, they excite us, they deepen our understanding of the ordinary. They make luminous. At their best, they contain what I call the timeless and the timebound.

Myths are the original ecstasies: tales ground down by the gleaming teeth of wolves, containing the whispers of a Ghanaian grandmother, fulsome with the blue longings of the moon. Such stories shouldn't behave or play nice. They slip the trap of allegory and pad off over the snow, leaving us baffled and delighted.

When they fulfill this mystical mandate, you get what could be called a Sacred Story. It's a tale that's not transactional but transformative, takes rupture and gives it rapture. It's what we've always done. From the very beginning of things we've tended to imagine in story. Thousands and thousands of years before cuneiform tablets, we stuffed wild, useful ideas into stories so they could be passed from generation to generation.

Of course, everything has its darker aspect. The word often associated with myth is *fiction*, a fib, a lie. For me this is a thin and inaccurate read. The nearest it could get to truth is the sense of modern advertising aggressively selling a story so hard its essential game plan is possession of your imagination. That's not where I'm going. That's a toxic mimic. That comes from a long tradition that assumes all stories are nutted out by human beings trying to orientate their way in the travails of life. It's effectively a secular position and is not mine, nor ever was. For more on that kind of thing, seek out Roland Barthes, sipping his coffee and scowling at trees.

The other position—shared by Indigenous and Celtic cultures alike—is that myths arise from going walkabout. That you take off. Shake the civilised off you. If you walk long enough a mountain may say something to you, a bird may sweep by with some gossip, you may lie down by a river and get dreamt. The human wasn't the centre of the imagining, but they were awfully good at picking up the news. It was an earth *that thought in myth,* and we used to have the smarts to interpret that heavenly braille. You get the difference, I'm sure. A myth worth its salt was not a lie but stood solid in divine ground. More than just human. It, in some tangible and mysterious way, spoke across species. A storyteller wasn't just an entertainer, they were in touch with the efficacious. This is not the same thing as an ad campaign for Nike telling us we can be anything we want. No. Myths tell us we are to be something quite specific.

Storytellers know there are many types of time. There's the kind that glows on your phone, there's the kind that pings and tells you that you have a Zoom call in ten minutes. The Greeks call that *Kronos* time, and it has its function. But there's another type—*Kairos,* which lifts us into the loftier dimensions of myth. We are back to the transactional and the transformative, the timebound and the timeless again. There's also once under a time, once around a time, once when there wasn't any kind of time at all. The worst thing in the world is to ask a teller to "get to the point."

Myth is about connotation not denotation; it's about symbols not signs. People are snooty these days about metaphors, but I'd say that's nonsense. A metaphor is a symbol that mercifully doesn't tell you quite what it is, allowing an indefinite number of associations to flood in. It's how poems work. It's how we find something to nest within when we fall in love. We need wiggle room for our imagination.

I could tell you that myth is a beautiful lie that tells a deeper truth; I could tell you that myth never was and always is; I could tell you myth is truth without the use of facts, but actually, *no,* even those diminish it, make it smaller somehow. After replying thousands of times to the question I will just settle with what I said at the beginning: *Myth is a Sacred Story.*

And some of the most sacred of those stories circle around the tale of a dying and resurrected king. Who carried a great burden for his people and turned that burden into an extraordinary act of love. And some of us believe that the most sacred story crash-bang-walloped into the kind of time we can all register, *ours.* Myth collides with history.

I've long held the strange idea that the arrival of Christ begins in the middle of Homer's *Odyssey.* When Odysseus visits the Underworld and Achilles tells him the following, the game is up for the old order:

"Sooner be a slave to a poor man than King of the Underworld."

With these words, from the greatest of Greek heroes, the world turns. Klaos—*imperishable glory*—is the deepest ambition of a warrior. When Achilles says it is without meaning down in Hades, something utterly new is being announced. A shield is hurled on a stone floor. A fresh consciousness. Yeshua, the God-Man is coming. *The last shall be first.*

So where to begin with the kind of myths I think we need? I want to bring in an idea that I've worked with for years as a wilderness guide. We could call it the Old Idea. That idea is that our soul—or most of it—lives outside our body. This is a big break with the Western notion of interiority as the primary poetic truth. Less of the therapy couch, "my truth," the interior franchise of fairy tales, *me, me, me.*

In the simplest terms it means we are profoundly connected to the stuff of earth—storms, roosters, oaks, pomegranates—but that a great withdrawing has taken place. A divorce. It seems the price for commercial expansion is a certain kind of imaginative pulling back, a concerted withdrawing of the wider, wilder, world-soul. With this in place, less consciousness and then less conscience is required from our actions. I'm not suggesting abandoning science and psychology completely, but I am sure that our very senses are hinting at something *bigger*. We are meant to take up more spiritual space. Matthew Arnold in his seminal poem "Dover Beach" lamented this evacuation by comparing a melancholy, roaring tide leaving the shore. But, of course, tides come *back*.

In a pre-Copernican world, *everything* was interior; we viewed our gods in star formations, even our very fates were writ large and circling over our heads. We were enclosed in soul. To see a grizzly at the water hole was to encounter a spirit; when thunder boomed it was because our heart was broken—*obviously*. Everything out there was telling us about *in here*. Our body was the beautiful, lonesome crossroads between the two.

We don't have unique access to our soul; it rests in condor nests and gambling dens in Russian villages, slipping back into our body with kohl-streaked cheeks just seconds before we wake up. It's not entirely human.

Far from being untruths, myths have traditionally been forefront in the shaping of human beings. They show us what to defend, what to care about, the need for pluck, sacrifice, and generosity. In the writ-largeness of their narratives we can locate our own stories, like a river finding the sea. They are a home for us. Some say they are our very bones. Parzival is now in my bones, my time with Black Elk too.

What are your bone stories?

2

ON BONES

The first old stories I heard were from church, from the big book. My dad was a young preacher and the house reverberated with whatever sermon he was currently coaxing into life. One of the most interesting chapters in the big book was the first one, Genesis, and I remember thinking a great deal about the following sentence:

"The Lord God formed the man from the dust of the ground and breathed into his nostrils the breath of life, and the man became a living being."[1]

I liked it. It was *weird*.

It seemed to say that we humans were mud people with a kind of holy breath that had swept through us. It seemed both earthy and elevated, both at the same time. As an image it seemed more like a cave painting than a Leonardo da Vinci sketch.

Thinking about this image for forty-five years I realise that I want to talk to the mud in us, and use holy breath to do so. That without that breath we may grow up into "something," but a human being it may not be. In a book about getting made, it's worth having a look at the initial ingredients.

When I think about mud in this way, I think about it signifying something essential. The *prima materia* of the human experience. But—in the language of medieval alchemy—we require the holy breath to turn the lead into a gold, and for us to become a "living being," as Genesis puts it. I think there have been moments in my life when I've barely been living at all. When we hear a myth it animates the mud of our condition. We get excited by such stories, we jump up and live, we weep, we laugh, we push through difficulty on the breath of a story. Without the breath there is no alchemy, we remain mud and only mud.

A mud life is all outcomes and no journey, is endless insurance but never a gamble; a mud life is a statement not a poem. It's only half the picture. A mud person is nervous of a dance floor, a poker game, a paradox. They are not entirely animate. On the other hand, I'd suggest that it's also the mud that grounds us, sobers us, cautions us when necessary. A person of too much breath and not enough mud is going to enjoy floating ecstasies but also crashing depressions. In Greek myth such a figure would be called a *puer aeternus*, and the mud person a *senex*. The puer is a little like Peter Pan; the senex is an old man or woman. In Russian fairy tales, the quality of the mud is represented by a talking horse who offers sage council; the holy breath shows up as a firebird, filled with light and excitement. The challenge is to stay in relation to both directives, the tension of the opposites.

In this question of getting made, handling tension is part of the process. In ancient Ireland a potential king or queen was taken to the hill of Tara and given a chariot with two strong-willed horses. The challenge was not to let the chariot be pulled one way or the other but dictate a third way that came from the dynamic of both. That required both extraordinary discipline and sublime improvisation from the potential sovereign. Qualities you could argue come from mud (discipline) and breath (improvisation) combined.

Flamenco is a dance of both spontaneity and well-organised steps. Georgia O'Keeffe conjured something both stark and lush in her paintings of flowers, skulls, and the desert. Technique and inspiration leap from hand to brush in her work, just like an old flamenco dancer swishing and clacking her dress and shoes on a wooden floor demonstrates a lifetime's devotion to her craft. We are witnessing a grown-up in that moment.

An old Anglo-Saxon phrase for aging is *the bone house*. The bone house creaks and slumps, stretches and contracts. Full occupancy of the bone house means acceptance of the complexity of aging, both its boons and diminishments. You'll know someone who's made that covenant by a certain wry humour, possibly a little dark. Wallace had something of that going on—one minute senatorial, the next gleeful as a child. Without voluntarily entering the bone house, we insult the architect of the whole affair and don't get properly made. The end result of a made human being is almost as varied as birds in the sky or fish in the oceans, but a few things usually serve as binding agents in the process. Duress, wonder, opportunity, and constraint.

And from a religious perspective we never get near getting made without submission to the energy that created the unfolding in the first place—God. We don't like the word *submission* these days. It cramps our wingspan, corrals our horses. *I* make those decisions, thank you very much. I held that position for almost fifty years and ran that rodeo for about as far as it could go. I don't anymore.

So I tell stories to feed the mud and breath in us. A myth is robust enough to hold the tension of the soul of mud, and the spirit of breath.

A myth is wily enough to know that it's the combination of mud's substance and breath's innovation that makes an interesting human being. To choose is to lose; the *complexity* is what God wishes for us.

In this chapter I'm going to show you how we could unpack a fairy tale without denuding it of its power. How its themes and symbols may have something to say about the mud and breath of our own lives. How it may say something about our relationship to God. We're going to start with one of my very favourites: a Scandinavian story that sometimes goes by the title "East of the Sun and West of the Moon."

———◦◦◦———

There once was a woman who fell in love with a bear.

The daughter of a king and queen, she lived with them and her two sisters in a castle. Although she resided in great luxury, she found life most thrilling when she wandered the woods. She ignored the castle's inner courtyard, filled with riches and playthings. Her sisters found this most unusual. One morning as she strolled, she came across a huge white bear lying on his back and playing with a golden wreath in his paws. He was Lord of the Animals. The girl had never wanted anything as much as she wanted that wreath. Plucking up courage, she offered him food and treasure in return for the wreath. He laughed and spoke, as bears could in those days. He said the only thing that would work as an exchange would be for her to leave her life in the castle and to come live with him in the forest. She was both terrified and intoxicated by the idea. She couldn't forget him, or the wreath.

She went and told her father the king. He gathered his silver-smiths, and they created a wreath for her, to dissuade her from leaving. But it didn't fit quite right, was not as elegant as the wreath she'd glimpsed out there in the wild. She couldn't be persuaded. Twice the king tried to disguise her older sisters to go with the bear, as older sisters marry first. But their disdain was obvious. When the bear arrived a third time at the drawbridge, she leapt on his back and plunged her nose into his fur, which smelt of apple blossom. He asked her, *Have you ever sat more comfortably than you do now, have you ever seen more clearly?*

Never in all my life was the response. With that, they departed into the depths of the forest.

THE ARRIVAL OF MAGIC

Fairy tales give a great deal in just a few sentences. We have someone born into comfort yet they yearn for more. We will never learn the young girl's name, partially because their name, really, is *ours*. The story is talking directly to some divine discontent in us, the readers. We—most of us—live with luxuries unthinkable to our ancestors. Yet we have an instinct as to why she would be wandering a forest. Adventure, the unexpected, the uncorralled.

Most stories begin with a break from the norm (we'll come back to this), the day that was nothing like the day before. This is the arrival of wonder. The trouble will come later.

Consequence will arrive. A decision has to be made. Do I risk my treasure, my stability, my stature for the sake of the golden wreath? And what exactly *is* the golden wreath?

The wreath is anything that pulls us from the steady life and the predictable outcome. It's a leap with no sense of quite where we will land. Its currency is thrill, risk, and expansion. It's a dizzying proposition that won't give you no rest.

Whenever there are three sisters or brothers, it's a hint that such a situation may come along more than once in our lives. We may refuse the wreath at twenty, or forty-five, but at sixty it's a matter of life and death. We may have stewed in the grinding reality of abdicating the adventure and the hollowed-out result of such a decision. Of course, I can't help but see Christ standing there, saying, *Come find out.*

There's also the fascinating detail of the false wreath; that when we are setting out on an adventure of true worth we will be offered a facsimile to seduce us, slow us in our tracks, turn us around. But a garden is not a forest, and a wreath made in a basement is not the same as the crown of the Lord of the Animals. So we are shown a master class in spirit (the girl's pluck); right now the story is still being drawn with clean, simple lines. But what will happen next?

—◦•◦—

It was a happy life they had. It turned out the bear lived in a castle himself, grander than her parents', not a cave filled with moss and bones. He even had a name: Valemon, high king of bears.

At night, in the darkness of their chamber, he became a man, taking on bear form when he left in the morning. Three times she became pregnant, and three times the babies were spirited away. It was a little dreamlike, the bear-castle. After a time she visited her parents to let them know all had turned out well, and her mother asked her what her beloved looked like: the colour of his eyes and hair. She confessed, *I don't know, I've never actually seen him.* With this her mother produced a candle and encouraged her to light it the next time he slept.

Well, on her return she lit the candle as he rested, but three drops of wax fell burning onto his throat. He leapt from the bed in pain and anger, becoming a bear again. *Because you did this I must leave and marry the Troll Queen of the East. I am enchanted. One more month and I would have been a man again, all the time!* He fled the chamber with her leaping on his back, but this time he tried to shake her off, until finally she was abandoned in the forest, as he disappeared into the night.

She could have returned to her parents but she elected to find him. For many hard months she wandered the forest. She grew thin, belly stuck to spine, assailed by hard dreams and regret, but she never gave up. After a long time she came across cottages, three in total. There she was given three gifts by three little girls and three old women: scissors that produced clothes just by snipping the air, a goblet that filled with any drink you desired, a cloth that produced any food you could imagine. She was learning how to clothe herself, to provide food and drink for herself in the most unsettling of conditions.

LIFTING THE CANDLE

Moving into this next section we encounter surprises. The bear is a noble and lives in a castle even greater than our parents'. There was no hint of this when we leapt on his back. And what is happening with the babies being spirited away? Why isn't there a great enquiry about it? Well, that's because this is a fairy tale, not a modern novel. It's a way the storyteller lets us know we are moving into a dreamlike reality of even deeper symbols and happenings. We are given space to just puzzle about these things; not every bow is neatly tied.

On Valemon: Maybe an idea we are chasing proves to be far more successful than the first early hints. We just follow our gut and suddenly it all pays off. We don't overthink things. But the years pass, and it remains an incomplete picture. It is right for the mother to give her daughter the candle. Without the candle the story is never pushed along, and we find ourselves stuck. We can birth something— the castle is fertile in a way—but we can't raise anything in that environment. It's betwixt and between.

I wonder if you've ever had the candle lit on you when you least expect it? Couples rarely agree to light it at the same time. One of us may well prefer the shadows. But without the candle we would never know that Valemon is actually betrothed to the Hag Troll Queen, is actually under some kind of enchantment. Some forms of information we will never volunteer unless it's forced from us.

From here on the hard yards begin, the initiatory ground so many of these stories illustrate. The honeymoon is long gone, you've been chucked from the back of your beloved, asked too many deep questions, and life has decided your great education is to unfold. These wanderings of the fairy forests can take long stretches in our own lives: Depression can take us there, illness, a drop in status, a creeping flatness that slowly overwhelms. You would imagine the false wreath never feels more attractive than at such a moment. There's admirable resolve present, and results are shown in the appearance of the three cottages. In a time of harrowing she is learning to clothe, nourish, and feed herself. In ancient Greece the cottages would have been temples. This is an awfully long way from the young girl who skipped out at the beginning of our story. She's becoming a woman acquainted with grief, fear, and stamina. *Lifting the Candle* is a life worth the examining. It's a gleam of consciousness that radiates in wider and wider orbits. And some of the things we'll see can be troubling. Waking up can be troubling.

Finally she came to the ice mountain of the Troll Queen, whose abode was on top of it. At the base, she came across a blacksmith's hut and gave drink and food to the hungry family, supplied them with warm clothes for the winter. In exchange, the blacksmith forged her a pair of iron claws. It was with these she could climb an unclimbable mountain. Surely, something in her was becoming bear.

The moment she arrived at the top of the mountain the Troll Queen appeared, magnificently terrible in appearance. *What are you doing in my place? What do you want?* The girl replied, *I was wondering, oh mighty one, what you would give your guests to drink at the wedding, for I have a goblet that would supply them endlessly with anything they would desire.*

The Troll Queen, who had only anticipated offering blood to her guests, desired the goblet. *In return for my goblet let me see your husband Valemon. I hear he is an extraordinary fellow.* The queen agreed, but she drugged him with a sleeping potion, so when the girl was allowed into his chamber he slept all night. She made the same arrangement with the cloth, and for a second night he slept on as she wept over him. So loud was her grief it was overheard by others who told Valemon the next day that there was a weeping woman in his chambers. He knew at once who this must be.

The next night he only pretended to swallow the sleeping potion. Even when the Troll Queen pierced his arm with an iron knitting needle, he did not stir. But when she left the chamber, he opened his eyes and was passionately reunited with the bear-woman, the wild third daughter. They nuzzled and wept so loudly they woke those sleeping next door again. They happened to be carpenters, and, happy at this reunion, offered to help the situation. The wedding was to involve the Troll Queen and her suitor walking across a wooden bridge to two thrones on the other side. There was a deep chasm in the mountain underneath. The carpenters had loosened a couple of planks in the bridge, towards the middle.

When the Troll Queen got there, she slipped from this story, down, down, and straight into another tale. For several days, the bear-woman became the Queen of the Mountain, until she and her husband decided to go back to marry in full view of her parents in the very first castle she grew up in. Because, despite their years together, *they had never been properly married.* As they passed each of the cottages where the queen had been gifted, it was revealed that each of the three girls was in fact a daughter of hers, spirited away to help her at her direst moment. Now all were reunited, and the little girls were her bridesmaids. What a wedding it was! Everyone you ever loved as a child was there, and all the animals you ever cared for. It took seven men working seven days just to stir the mustard! Firebirds danced, musicians played, and everyone was in love, even the long married. And as far as I know, Valemon and the bear-woman reside to this day, gracious and giving to their people.

NO FREE LUNCH

It's important to understand in our story that the Hag Troll Queen is not a demon. There's actually something rather endearing about her on occasion. She has oomph. A psychologist might suggest that a descent like the one the daughter endured will sift to consciousness a powerful figure like the queen. That's a little neat for me, a little domestic, but it may chime. Other therapists might see the queen as "knowledge of one's personal shadow," but again, I prefer the Hag

Troll Queen *as* the Hag Troll Queen. But the detail that the daughter becomes the queen of the mountain before they leave is important. She carries more sass, more wit, more knowledge, more sobriety, more swagger than when she first set out as a princess. Something has been integrated, not exactly defeated.

We recall the bartering with the goblet and the cloth. Things are almost never free in the tales. As we go through life, Underworld qualities give us our credibility—think a John Lee Hooker or a Frida Kahlo. We believe these people. The crow has marked their face and we trust them accordingly. The Underworld is a mythic shorthand for the most testing part of the initiatory tale. Without them we would never have a husband, just a lover.

Without the journey we never have the gifts—remember when the daughter feeds and clothes the blacksmith's children? There is an extraordinary clue as to the curation of suffering here. Not to fetishize pain or become addicted to scars, but to know that duress can—sometimes—lead us to the palace of wisdom. It can lead to us being able to bless others, rather than being twisted up in our own neurosis or self-absorption. At the start of the story the daughter could have given the blacksmith's children coin or baubles, but here she provides them with far more. It's an earned gifting now. This is a story that began with wonder but took us through travail and ultimately wisdom. There's a reason why we always circle back to such stories. They are seeded in the lived experience of all humans; it's why they ring true. In a startling way the whole tale is a courtship, with the chance of an abiding marriage only really present at the very end. And the end provides the joy of the three emerging daughters— that what we birthed in the early stages can now be fully engaged in our lives, and the final detail that the marriage takes place at the castle at the beginning. Not as a compromise, but as sign of completion, wholeness, and a centre invigorated by relationship to the edge. The "mud" of the daughter's sober maturation has aided the pluck of her lively "breath," and she now finally abides as both a sovereign and a wife. This process absolutely qualifies as what we could call an initiation. In the next chapter I will map out a little of what initiation can look like through the symbols and structures of a fairy tale.

ON INITIATION

We all have them: moments of crisis or opportunity, sometimes the terror-wallop of both at the same time. We can sail on steady winds, then suddenly the weather turns and the map flies from our hand. These are the dread or blissed encounters that by their very pressure can be the making of us. These are life's initiations. Illness, scandal, demotion; seen through a mythic lens these are hard instructors. If you can bear it they are going to school you. This isn't to imply we should go looking for scars, but remain open to learning when trouble shuffles along.

What I'm going to do now is show in myth how this often reveals itself: through a set of stages. I'll give the elements of this progression the rather grand titles of Severance, Threshold, and Return, or what we could think of as *leaving the familiar, encountering the numinous, returning with a gift*. I'll present it like a story.

There was a life you once had. It was probably rather nice. Maybe not that exciting, but you knew where you stood. If you were very lucky it was something of a Shire, and it felt stable and confirming. You look around the settlement and see many contented faces, many folks that had never left the place. But it's going to be different for you.

Because something is coming that will bust you out, reluctantly or otherwise. You will break from the familiar. This is the bit called Severance. A threat comes to what you know. It may arrive as a war, an illness, a spiritual crack-up, a betrayal, a scandal, any number of things that shake what you thought you knew. A word arrives that the scriptwriters cherish: jeopardy. You lose your hands, a dark power circles the village, trouble has arrived. The initiatory summons has arrived and you have to set out, no matter how your legs totter. The quest for wisdom begins.

What you find will be what my old friend, the late Malidoma Somé, called *the world turned upside down*. It will be disorientating, visionary, illuminating, and hopefully rewarding. You may bump into a realm called the Underworld, or someplace else called the Otherworld—there's any number of terms—the more localised the better, in my opinion. There may be a journey—by sea or land—involving monsters, temptations, all sorts. Hair-raising. You are going to get stretched, deepened, walloped by the ghastly, redeemed by the holy. There will be moments when it appears all hope is lost, and you have to experience what it feels like to continue to exist within that hopelessness. This is the time of Threshold.

It can be baffling, depressing, a wasteland or a sea storm, but you will be rewired in some fashion. And you will likely bring two things back. Things that may seem very different but are completely entwined. A limp and a gift. Threshold marks you, can even seem like a diminishment in the eyes of the world—hence the limp—but only within its deepening can you articulate the gift. No matter how charismatic you are, people don't quite trust you until they know you've been through Threshold. You remain a chatty young hopeful, ill at ease with silence, loss, and any kind of convincing empathy. Threshold can last a while. You could be meeting the Devil at the Crossroads, or down in the belly of a fish.

Ultimately, after the wrestling with an angel, or Baba Yaga, or some great bear god deep in a mountain, you are to return. Something you found through your knowledge-of-peril is to distil into something called wisdom. And that wisdom provides a key, a picture, a boon, a balm for whatever suffering sent you out in the first place. Without carrying a gift for others there is no Return, and the initiatory process I've just laid out remains incomplete. It's a two-step not a three-step programme. Like an elastic band snapping you are continually pulled back into Threshold, which only seems to provide *trauma not treasure.* It is location and manifestation of the gift as much as a good therapist that moves one on from this.

Severance, Threshold, Return, this is what I believe we remember down in our mud bodies. And when our lives—religious or otherwise—don't reflect this primordial pattern, something in us remains antsy. Distracted. Not getting scratched where we most defiantly itch.

The churches are emptying because we are not speaking to the mud and holy breath in us. We are forgetting the epic story we are tuned for. The adventure has somehow got lost. Irony of ironies of bloody ironies, Christianity is regarded by millions of people as safe, boring, and pedestrian.

I've been reading the First Nations Version of the New Testament, and whilst staying loyal to the Gospels we are familiar with, it has floored me. By using titles that sit truer to Indigenous culture, another kind of electricity starts to bubble up. Jesus becomes *Creator Sets Free,* Jacob is *Heel Grabber,* Mary Magdalene is *Strong Tears,*

Bethlehem is *House of Bread*. You are hearing the old story but with the lethargy sloughed off its hide. Suddenly you are asking, maybe for the first time in an age, *What happens next? Creator Sets Free* stands with *Stand on the Rock* (Peter) by the *Sea of Rolling Water* (Sea of Tiberias) and all the poetry floods back into the picture. It's not reinventing the story to appease and appeal to a society that barely gives a hoot for it anyway, but it's reconnecting with artistry and imagination the mud/breath essence of our secretive, mythic hearts. This is a joyful labour we could, all of us, be getting behind.

Our lives *are* mythic, but we lack more and more the sacred braille to read it so. So much of life is not what happens but what we *do* with it. The more existential it becomes, the more of a Hercules complex we develop. Myth is a relational field, a contact sport, it seeks connection, and most importantly it wishes us to deepen. As Paul says, first you have milk but then you need meat.[1] The way we understand as a beginner is not how we understand as a veteran.

It's possible you could attempt a spiritual life but stay firmly entrenched in the Shire. We renege on the call. Millions do. We have a cosy, cookie-cutter, one-size-fits-all, long-entrenched, batten-down-the-hatches belief. But what can happen with that? We never die *before we die*. We never don't *not know*. Sometimes we have to get *lost*.

The absence of that means No Threshold. That means no return, no transformation, not really. I don't know how we get much in the way of Holy Spirit if we never set out to begin with. In a functioning initiation you would likely be given new clothes at the Return stage, or some intrinsic totem to show you are not the same. Something happened.

When I sit by the fire, folks don't always like it when I peer through the smoke at them, drop the small talk, and say, *What part of you has come to die?*

COLOURS OF A FAIRY TALE

We've talked about Sacred Stories, mud and holy breath, and the *Severance, Threshold, Return* progression that often runs through such tales. Now I want to bring in three colours you find of great significance in many stories. Red, Black, and White. They have qualities associated with them that also flesh out something of the getting-made process within myth. These colours are the fruits of the initiatory journey.

The colours are often located in fairy tales, famously the Grimms' tale "Iron Hans," where a young man rides three horses into three battles: a black horse, a red horse, a white horse. Something in us just wakes up when these colours get close to each other. What I'm going to do first of all is make associations between the colours and their attributes, in doing so drawing on the work of my old mentor Robert Bly. I've been teaching it so long it's etched into my own life experience, but it's always good to gesture back to the well where you first drank the water.

The Red is to do with life force, power, survival, grandeur, ego. If you are lucky it comes online somewhere in childhood and you have it readily available as a kind of fuel. It's the Red that urges you on, gives you the courage to take a position, draw a line in the sand. It's the Red that lets you dream big, pack a suitcase, and head out on an adventure. Someone in the Red is not crippled with self-doubt but can act decisively in their ambition to get ahead. Ambition is the key word here. It's an individualistic position not a community one, not really. It's about breaking from the pack and winning the race. It's about working up a headful of steam and receiving the praise. The Red likes an audience. The Red will help you pull an all-nighter finishing an essay and also remember to do the footnotes and bibliography.

It's energised by grades. It's rare to have a successful career in the West without ready access to the Red. You are in touch with your body's needs, your desire, and the promise of reward.

The flip side of the Red (and all these colours have them) is self-obsession, arrogance, aggression, a distinct lack of care for others, "don't tread on me." Without mentoring, the Red can create a warlike personality or community. With mentoring, someone in the Red can really get things done for the good. They kick ass once they cop on to the notion of service. Without the Red you will struggle to get the book finished, the move completed, the project launched.

The Black is to do with failure, descent, vulnerability, melancholy, and self-knowledge. It's not about what worked but what didn't. If the Red can be associated most acutely with youth, the Black tends to become more visible in middle age. The Black indicates Underworld experience. The road gets awfully crooked somewhere in your forties or fifties. There could be a divorce in the mix, or a scandal, or some kind of low-lying depression you just can't shake. There's a baby you never had, a job you never got, an illness that knocked you completely off centre. It could be that you achieved all you could in the Red and then found that it didn't give you what you hoped it would. Even success can be a gateway to the Black. The Black is to do with your cock not working, distance from friends, listlessness, lack of libido, inability to really concentrate, projects half completed.

But. And it's a big *but.* Without the Black we really don't understand empathy. It's why in the Grail epic of Parzival, he doesn't know the question to ask the ailing Fisher King the first time he meets him. He's all about the Red and knows nothing about the Black yet. That deeper knowledge is years away. The Black can make us an awfully good listener, more discerning, more compassionate, and with a rather unruly sense of humour. We know about disaster, and yet, here we are, the old woman cackling away, salty and deep.

Without the Black we have little to say about shipwrecks, blizzards, and getting lost in the fog. Without the Black we have intelligence but we don't really have wisdom. If you are guided in ways to curate the Black you can become sage-like; if you don't you can become terribly bitter. To judge the Black by the Red's standards is the shortcut to even greater misery.

The White is to do with community, not frantic individuation. It has stayed connected to both the energy of the Red and the depth of the Black and now wants to work with both for the good of a wider earth. It's the colour not just of ambition, not just of grief, but of service. Neither of the previous stages evaporate but are harnessed now to a less self-centred orientation. The White is that precious ground of eldership, of carrying the ability to bless, to raise up others, to encourage. It's not needy. It is the breast that is full of milk. It's absolutely generative, it doesn't cling, it's neither sour nor excessively sweet, it sees calmly and for long, long distances.

You can feel that this most appropriately seems to land in older age. But we can move in and out of all these colours depending on where life takes us. I know women in their seventies filled with the Red, and kids of fifteen chucked in the Black; sometimes there's a twenty-five-year-old with a calm assurance we all gravitate towards. Though in broad strokes you could say this fits the general progression of life—youth, midlife, old age—most of us also flit between them as we age.

I remember Bly saying to me that he thought the West celebrated the Red and the White pretty well, but really didn't know what to do with the Black. The appalling lack of care for our returning veterans was an example of that. That we didn't really know how to grieve publicly, and that we walked backwards even into our own dying. That we would have our leaders skip from Red to White and avoid the Underworld entirely.

Another association with the colours leads us to two big words I've been using: spirit and soul. Red is a spirit road, a "yes we can" moment, an "I am Spartacus" rousing of the self. The Black is a soul road, a "maybe we can't" reflection, a "road less travelled" deepening of the soul. The two qualities are not quite the same. And it's the White in us that knows when and how to respond with either spirit or soul.

In the Greek tale of *Psyche and Eros* we get a tremendous weaving of spirit and soul and a portrayal of how much they need each other. Eros is the brightness of spirit, Psyche the darkening of soul, and we see how absolutely in love one is with the other. But to be together, both must undertake long, arduous, and very sobering tasks. Only then does Aphrodite bring them back together, after something of a harrowing. I think she wants to ensure a long, old marriage for her son Eros.

I think of Yeshua in the Red trashing the Temple; Yeshua in the Black drawing in the dust and saying, *Whoever is without sin cast the first stone*; Yeshua in the White saying shalom to his disciples even after they scattered at his crucifixion.

There's a story I've told for years: "Tatterhood," about a woman who can't conceive. A wise old woman gives her advice that involves consumption of a white flower. She warns her, however, that there will also be a red flower nearby, and that she should not, under any circumstances, consume it. Well of course she does, and then she consumes the white and gives birth to twins, one who's wild as the pale moon. It took a decade of teaching it before I realised that both those flowers are cradled in a third that is never mentioned: the dark earth. Boom. The three colours. Without the dark, the Red and White never grow.

It's worth doing a little self-diagnosis on your own nutrient-rich relationship to the three colours. Is there a lack somewhere? Or an excess? Remember they are something of an alchemical experiment, volatile in nature. Your loved ones will know of the spillage. You yourself are the vessel. I think I've known a fair bit of the Red and the Black, but have balked at the White. I've gone a bit blank there. Storytellers say always to pay attention to where in a story your attention vacates the scene: That's the place to circle back and attend to. What do you not want to see? Which horse do I need to ride at this point in my life? When I write a book I always draw on the three colours: the Red to maintain the sheer willpower and eros to get it done, the Black to humanise the endeavour—bring in the limp as well as the gallop—and finally the White to expand the picture past a self-centred narrative and into the light of something that could be communally useful. But we should never quite lose touch with what any of the colours represent; they flare us up or simmer us down appropriately. Some of us can be a little scared of showing the Red, but it can be needed at times. I'll finish this chapter with a story that shows it.

Once upon a time the Buddha was walking across India, and he came to a dragon that had consumed many people at the gates of a city. People were terrified. The Buddha conversed with the serpent, convinced him to stop taking lives. Amazingly the dragon agreed. Happily the Buddha continued on his way. Years later, the Buddha was passing the city and decided to drop by on his friend the dragon. The dragon was in an awful state. People were driving their carts and animals right over him to get into the market. He'd lost scales, his skin had lost its sheen, he was a mess. Buddha spoke:

My friend, this is terrible! What happened?

I did what you said, I stopped killing people.

It's true, I told you to stop killing, but I never said to stop growling!

A little teaching story on the Red, right there.

In the next chapter we will approach an area that lends itself utterly to getting made: namely, our relationship to death. This is the first of several essential themes to do with growing into a real human being.

4

ON DEATH

It's not my time. That was the phrase that had ensured the workshop leader's gatherings were packed from one side of the globe to the other. She'd come back from a near-death experience and a sudden cease-and-desist on what had seemed till that moment to be a terminal illness. But no. The woman had—doctors attested—made a complete recovery after her experience. She now had all sorts of heavenly tips for those in similar predicaments. Understandably, the room was filled with desperate people, hoping that by proximity to her some of that back-from-the-brink medicine would rub off on them.

The problem was the woman was nowhere to be seen.

Two days in, she'd taken the afternoon off and was having a spa somewhere nearby with her husband. I received a rattled call from the supervisors and reluctantly accepted the request to hold the ailing fort till she deigned to return. I gingerly picked my way through the oxygen machines and wheelchairs and had a good look at the people. They'd had forty-eight hours now of miracle-speak, and they didn't seem to be exactly buoyant. I asked for a few windows to be opened, then said the first thing that came into my head.

OK. The title of this afternoon's little adventure is this: "Maybe It Is My Time."

They didn't recoil—at least visibly—and so I began to tell them a fairy tale. It was one from the dark end of the street, with ten different types of depth to it. I remember they valiantly stayed with it, even seemed relieved that through the wider lens of a story they could be held in the forest of the condition they were actually in. That they could talk about what often seems a great Western heresy: *that things end.* That our lives, in the shape we know about, will finish.

After the workshop I drove back to Charlotte's bedside. Charlotte was at the end of her life, a young woman riven horribly by breast cancer, with kids and a husband. I wended my way through the oddly quiet house, with its curtains drawn and toys everywhere. I went up the stairs to the small room she was in. I'd visited her several times, times when we could still just about chat, but that was past now.

She was absolutely skeletal, and her once lustrous hair was a delicate little fuzz over her pale scalp. Her family had thought to move her to the workshop, to be one of the assembled hopers, but mercifully saw that moment had passed. So now she was nested in and fixing to die.

Getting here, to this moment, had taken a couple of years, so there was a kind of rag-worn acceptance about it. The room cleared out for a bit and I sang quietly to her, songs that may get sung when you are acknowledging a settling peace and that it's quite OK to move from one good place to another good place. Charlotte's kids were at school, and it seemed as if she wouldn't go till they got home. Sure enough, they returned, and sure enough, she soon died.

Her body remained in wake for several days downstairs. It was visited daily by her children, Charlotte having been carried down by her husband, father, brother, and myself. Musicians played, poems got read, and there was a revolving door of visitors from all over Europe. People sometimes fell asleep where they sat, under coats. The mood of the home was extraordinary—thin would be the word—and the day came when we sealed the handmade coffin with heated beeswax, the family singing the words *Good where I've been, good where I'm going to*, over and over.

Charlotte's mother-in-law was a priest and led the funeral. I had a fire lit and told a few stories. I remember men losing their stirrups carrying armfuls of flowers, women holding each other and staring into a hole cut into the side of Devon hill on a freezing spring day. I can tell you that Charlotte's death caused such an appropriate tear in our little community, it felt like we all scattered for a few years.

I salute the workshop leader and her recovery, but I loathe the addictive pungency of what such stories can do to us. Walking backwards into our own graves, so filled with denial because we lived not really once thinking that such a thing could one day happen to us. We miss the needed consciousness that sitting with a dead body will sober and sanctify us into. We haven't been done a favour by having the end of life ushered out of sight.

Part of getting made is the final part. Getting unmade. That preparing for death is not the same as what was before it. Denial is not just a river in Egypt. *It's not my time* is not the appropriate mantra of a grown-up. *One day, any day, it will be my time*, is better.

Years later I would be back on that hill, for another funeral, but we have not come to that story yet. A story to situate us is called "Grandfather Death."

Once upon a time, a worn-out man with thirteen kids was walking a lonely road. He met a man and asked him to be a godfather for the most recent, just to keep an eye out. The stranger revealed that he was, in fact, God, walking the earth in the cool of the day. Finding out he was God, the worn-out man changed his mind, as he felt God had allowed this grievous poverty. He walked on and asked another man. This grinning fellow was Old Scratch himself, the prince of this world, the Devil. Even though the Devil offered gold, the father took back the offer and hurried on. Finally the man met Death out there on the road. Because death took from both rich and poor, the father thought this fair, and asked him to be the godfather. Death tilted his head in the half-light and agreed.

When the thirteenth child became a young man, Death appeared at the edge of the woods one afternoon and beckoned him in. Death quietly showed the boy rare herbs and told him to become a healer by gaining knowledge of them. Death said when the boy was with a patient, if Death appeared at the top of the bed, then the boy should give herbs, but if Death appeared at the bottom, then the boy was to prepare the family for a death.

For a long time, this was how it went. The man grew in knowledge and then by reputation, and he was faithful to reporting wherever Death appeared, either at the top or the bottom of the bed. He was loyal to Death.

One day, a rich and powerful king was sick, and something got into the healer. He just seemed too auspicious, too powerful to let fade. When Death appeared at the bottom of the bed, in a flash the healer moved the bed so it appeared Death was at the top. The man quickly fed the king the herbs, and he did in fact recover.

Death warned him that if he tried that again he would end the boy's life.

Time passed and they travelled the kingdom together, assisting where they could. Some died, some recovered; Death never explained why it went one way or the other. Years later they found themselves back at the king's castle again. The mood was grave as the daughter of the king was now terribly sick. The king vowed half the kingdom and her hand in marriage if she could be saved. For the second time, something got into the healer; the riches were too great. As Death appeared at the bottom of the bed, again he swiftly moved the bed so Death was at the head. The boy hurriedly stuffed herbs in the daughter's mouth, and she did indeed recover.

Death doesn't bluff.

The boy found himself in a cave, surrounded by countless thousands of flickering candles. Death stood by him, pointing out that all the candles were at different lengths depending on how much time they had left to live. Death pointed out a nearby candle, explaining to him that this was the boy's, and there was barely any left. The lad begged to live, to be with his queen to ensure she bore a child. Said Death:

For a new candle to be lit, an old one must be extinguished.

Without thinking, the healer cried, *Put an old one out for the new life! If the queen has a child then it must live!*

Death agreed and snuffed out the healer's candle.

Not cheating death is a theme that rears up in ancient cultures, but now, in the words of my friend Stephen Jenkinson, we are so "death-phobic" that we wouldn't dream of bequeathing the notion that we may have a designated set of years and no more. Even a hundred years ago we would have seen many more deaths and at much younger ages. I would likely have died at nine of my burst appendix.

This fear—that I often share—of death demolishes the notion of dying being almost or exactly a skill, a passage that is not entirely and utterly a travesty. Not knowing quite what happens next scares us. It just does. We can read spiritual utterances designed to unruffle our tail feathers, but they rarely last at 3 a.m. when you've just found a lump. For all the wars, betrayals, and drive-by depressions, this is still a fascinating world. There's an awful lot to look at, to learn about, to serve. To be plucked out of all of that seems like losing hold of a miracle, at least to me. Heaven is a woodpile, family and friends, whisky and a cigar, standing by the back door gazing up at Orion. It takes an awful lot to convince me that there's something waiting that trumps that, I'm afraid. There's a reason we rage against the dying of the light. I do my best with the Christian picture, but sometimes I am a bear with little brain and it just seems too abstract to hang my heart on.

But this has begun to change. It came, as things often do with me, through a dream. I was in the middle of a retreat on Inis Oírr, the smallest of the Aran Islands, off Ireland. It was deep winter, and most folk were on the mainland.

In the dream I'm in a bedroom with an old lady, a relative. There's a servingwoman attending to her. I wish I could remember her more clearly, but she is tall, middle-aged, graceful. Fine eyes. In fact, her eyes are so extraordinary that my whole consciousness shifts. Like something I've not seen in this world. It's very hard to explain. She suggests I may want to have a break from the attending.

I move out of the small quarters and into a large room of ancient books and scribes, which then opens into a gargantuan hall, vast, many times bigger than an aircraft hangar. It's filled with things I love: huge urns from Crete painted with spirals, Viking longships, all sorts. But it's not like a museum where everything is self-consciously placed: Everything still seems alive and in movement. There are people and there is music. It's overwhelming and I start crying in the dream. And not just a tear. I'm privy to something, the movement of people, even cultures snaking through an enormous period of time. And what they made of their years here on earth. And behind everything I mentioned are swooping birds, and blue-grey hills, just like I love.

I retrace my steps through all this glory, past the torches and the scribes and the deerhounds, back to the little room where the dying is happening. When I come back I am only with the old lady for a few minutes before she turns in on herself, and breathing stops altogether. I realise I am not alone in the room.

The woman who I thought was the serving maiden takes a paintbrush, and with a chalky pigment, paints white rings around a cup of water the old woman had by the bed.

It was beautiful to be in the hall with all the things I love, but it was so very deep to be with the servingwoman. It's the most wonderful, peaceful feeling. I am delighted to have had this dream. There is no foreboding.

Later I am in the island's tiny shop, and a bird swoops onto the shelf of biscuits above me.

Ah, her, says the girl behind the counter.

I've known since then there's something ill-formed about my fear of death. An incompleteness. That there may be a consciousness vaster and sweeter and more profound than my fireside, my whisky, my friends. I was allowed to "feel" the difference for a few minutes. It may be that this wrestle with death is the thing that finally, testingly, brings us most profoundly to adulthood. Something changed in my father when he journeyed with cancer for several years. He grew roots somehow. He deepened.

The dream I had said to me: *This world can be a wonder but be not afraid of leaving it.*

When I am afraid, I call into the wilderness of dark that God is my staff and rod and comforter; when I am afraid, I remember the man who says he is the resurrection and the life, that though we die we do not die; when I am afraid, I remember citizenship in heaven. I call like the owl in the darkness for my cry to hit the confirming flank of my deliverer, and they hoot back. From fragile wisps these words have grown to become something of vine and bloom for me. Things of muscle and proclamation.

In every case of someone close to me dying, I have been disorientated and bereft. It's never been OK. I loathe that idea. In one way we continue on together, imaginatively, but there will always come a day when I know they live on now only in the crucible of memory. You will locate them in their absence more, far more, than their presence. I want to be more gracious to that emptiness, more understanding of it. More tender with it, more curious about it, on the days that I can bear it. And when I can't, I howl, and weep and drink and sleep.

In the weeks after Charlotte's funeral, she still felt close, still threaded constantly into conversations, into our tears and toasts, our hot anger and our willowed sorrow. That was as it should be. Maybe the dead leave slowly, just a footstep at a time, so the day—months or years after the funeral—when we realise with utter knowing we won't see them again in this world, is when they've moved beyond the orbit we've been desperately struggling to adjust to. Of course, Jesus turns to the thief on the cross and says that they will be together in Paradise. But that's the dead's business; we are left with signs and feelings, instincts and dreams. We always have been.

I've always wanted a lot chucked in the ground with me when it's time. Wagons, gold, great fanfare. Well, a bit of fanfare is fine, but not the accoutrements. As the Irish say, I will be *setting out on the trail of truth*, and you only get seeded for such a life in the moment of your death, funnily enough. We are ceremony people, we are story people, we are poetic people, and when the curtain in the Temple is ripped, that is our moment to make beauty in the face of our wounded appalment and death. We are spun into the light of life's feasting hall, and we are spun out again into the consecrated darkness. Like a little bird we slip through the doors and get dragged into love affairs and peculiar ambitions and moments of charity, and suddenly a woman with kindly eyes is painting circles on a cup, like the lines of a tree, and we are back out into some kind of next adventure. Not as Christians, as souls scattered into luminous fragments apart from our body, but reborn, but without those dreadful knees and high blood pressure. I can do with a bit of that. I remember these things, turn them like my prayer rope, in the sour hours of my doubt.

My friends over in the Other Place keep an eye out for me; they just do. They influence me, I think, make me braver, less naïve, keep me cleaving away to something essential. Sometimes I feel I have more over there than I do over here. I like to tell them, because I'm sure they're listening, that their faces are remembered. The books they wrote, their craic, their oomph or fathomless quiet. But I don't think they really mind so much either way, not anymore. It's an endless reflection of my grief for them and how that grief always ripens into love.

One of the things I really enjoyed about my aged pals was how outrageously pissed off they could get. Peevish eruptions that their younger iterations would never have dared display. There seemed more eccentricity, more devil-may-care, and far more truth-telling. Part of it was the sheer weird exhilaration that their canoe was about to dip over the falls. There'd be more tears, more sentimentality, more attack, like different gods attempting to flood their system: Zeus trying to hold it all together, Dionysus laughing at the chaos, Hermes trying to recount a naughty tale, Hera trying to call everyone to supper, forgetting there's only tins of beans and they are months out of date. These complexes could in the space of an hour resemble nothing less than a battlefield. Then slump: quiet, days by the fire sucking sweets. The old ones are gradually trying to make peace with what two decades back would have been unbearably undignified.

My old and late friend Malidoma Somé, an African shaman, said that the really antique villagers would become deliberately unkempt, sitting dirty and naked, as a sign that they soon were to become dust again. They sat like that and life continued on around them. In that village he told me that when a baby cries for the first time, everybody calls back, even the goats, and the baby gets claimed. He said you can't become an adult without that first affectionate shout back. He saw the West as drowning in that exact deficit. Maybe if you have that at the beginning of life it is easier to move into the ending of life.

Through this little story it seems like we aren't born quite right and we don't die quite right. That there needs to be more affection, more magical thinking, more display, more emotion at the beginning and end of our passage. We have to deal with the rest, not being able to remember the birth and dreading the departure. But *more* seems to be the essential word. We are haunted when we let our people die poorly. Not them, us.

There was a boy I knew—I loved him, we all did. Torin. We knew he likely wouldn't get much past twelve. He was the genius of our parish, really—big old eyes and shamanically piercing questions. He loved stories and he loved singing, especially a wonderful song about a firebird. Every now and then he would get sick, and he and his family would spend months in Bristol or Torbay Hospital. It was shattering for all of them each time. Around the time predicted, he was struggling more than usual, tubes in places where they really shouldn't have to be. The question was, *Should he be told?*

Kids know far more than they let on, most of the time. Every now and then he and I would meet and we would talk about fairy tales, myth, and sometimes heaven. I volunteered a few details about how I'd like to be buried and, casually asked him if he'd ever thought about such details. Without missing a beat, he turned his sage-like eyes on me and told me yes, he had such thoughts and he was now going to tell me about them. He used to announce things in that rather formal, adorable way.

He wanted to be buried in a place where he could be visited and there could be picnics. It was to be not too near the woods, as he didn't want people to get lost trying to find him. We talked about heaven. He said in heaven he would have no more pain and he would be able to ride horses with his friends. Barely able to breathe with emotion, I just nodded. When I recovered myself, I said that sounded just like heaven.

When he died, he, like Charlotte, was put in wake in his bedroom, on ice, wrapped in his Harry Potter cloak. Friends came flooding in, lost their minds, wept, sang, went deep quiet, got properly daubed in the magnitude of the unfolding. Handsome fella, always. It was a freezing winter day, his funeral. His coffin was placed in a flower-filled kayak, and with his family accompanying him, he was taken down the River Dart to the resting ground. Low mist, shell-shocked parents, kayaks filled with children and endless flowers, the lad's coffin. Crying, crying, singing, singing, then absolute quiet. Standing on the bank it was like seeing something from an entirely different age.

At the funeral I had two entirely different tasks. One was, in the face of his family and relatives, to somehow give due poetic and heartfelt diligence to the boy they loved so very, very much. For a few minutes he was to walk amongst us again, wind his way through us, ask his questions, gaze up with his Merlin eyes, ask us again about the business of living. In that frozen horseshoe of three hundred people watching, we needed more than the boy as a totem, we needed his scent again. Something had to thunder into the ice of that moment. Some element of him was to be unarguably alive.

Some attempt at that undergone, and songs sung, we moved to the second station. We looked into a dark, deep hole in the side of a freezing Devon hill, and we had to know something else.

We had to know that this beautiful boy was unarguably dead.

We had to look and look and look, still head-bangingly unaccepting that Death stood absolutely amongst us. The lad was at his Platform Nine and Three-Quarters, and his trail of truth had begun. Somewhere he was riding a horse and laughing, but not here, not with us, not at that moment. We were to stand shoulder to flagging shoulder in the tsunami of his absolute and shuddering absence.

A real human being, someone who's got made, has to live with the reality of both conditions at the same time. To lean too strongly one way or the other is to lose the tension of the truth at the heart of the opposites.

We all stayed on the hill in the cold and the grey for a long time. I am not the same.

Be like Charlotte's or Torin's family in the face of death. Be extravagant and protracted and real in your grief. Don't worry about doing it wrong. Labour over the preparation, exhaust yourself, show up. Make something by hand. Read stories to the beloved, allow yourself to go numb to it all. Fall asleep, get up, rinse and repeat. But don't let a chance like this go by. This is a time outside of time, and extraordinary things can happen. The Other Place is much closer.

Dress better as your old ones may be watching. Get a few grey hairs and don't think about plucking them out. Derailment is mandatory, but not to be forced. Make sure people see the body if they possibly can. Don't expect anything to be the same, even when folks stop dropping off pasta dishes at the door. You have entered a new, deepened world now. It has something to say to you.

It seems Death is the great integrity maker of us all, if we agree to bend our heads. There is some terrible deficit in the way many of us are born into this world, and it seems there is an equal absence in many of our departures.

I remember a story about Wallace Black Elk. It was noticed that one of his long plaits was dangling untidily while the other was ordered and neat. It rather ruined his look.

Why so? he was asked. *My wife is dead*, he replied, as if it required no further answer.

And of course, it didn't.

5

ON PASSIVITY

I would see him in the line after book events, often waiting to the very end so he could ensure the longest stretch telling me about his latest idea. I liked Jim; he was a hearty sort and had loyally followed my work for years. You'd have to be distinctly miserly to resent these brief monologues. But over time I'd noticed something. There was a "failure to launch" scent coming off him. He always had big plans but little sense of how to implement them. Jim had half a website built for his hoped-for business as a life coach. Jim had a great idea for a book and when he had some funding was going to write it. Jim was going to take a break from working in the supermarket and go walk the Camino. Well, time had passed and the website remained unfinished, the book unwritten, and I could still find him at the supermarket.

One evening I felt I owed Jim more than platitudes, more than vague encouragement. I told him that he was titillated by the fantasy of success—in whatever way that manifested—but lacked the fidelity of vision to really bring it into actuality. It's hardly uncommon; part of my accuracy of diagnosis was that I'd seen it in myself on occasion. For every intention we have, there's usually an equally strong counter-intention hidden just underneath the surface. I asked him what hidden contract he had made to stay exactly where he was, year after year. He seemed dismayed, but I asked him to stay in touch with me over the coming year. To be accountable to his ambition, to set dates, to keep me in the loop as his friend. Bring his fantasies into the daylight and make reality assist imagination. He shuffled off into the dusk and I wasn't sure I'd see him again. And for a while I didn't.

Finally a postcard. From the Camino. No website, no book, but walking, walking, walking. As he reminded me, the poet Antonio Machado says, "There is no road, we make the road by walking it." Jim had walked his way out of one of the most crippling hindrances to becoming a real, grown human being; he walked out of passivity. A year later a beautiful little book of poems and woodcuts dropped through my letter box, all about his journey. Treasure.

And passivity is not the terrain of people who never leave their parents' basement; there's a difference between passivity and sloth. Sloth can be kicked into touch fairly quickly with the right approach. Passivity is trickier, harder to locate because in certain areas of life we may be visible and active. I remember a friend who was a mover and shaker by day but absolutely passive on return to their partner. In fact he would endure a relationship without physical intimacy or much sense of shared vision. All the creativity and chutzpah was squared off, and they regressed to a child state behind closed doors, suitably miserable.

I remember the writer John Lee saying passive people were always half in and half out—that was something to check within ourselves. And the louder they protest what they want, some inner saboteur makes sure it doesn't happen. The conditions are never quite right. The passive person waits for the right moment to somehow break the spell, then they can make the big moves, just you wait and see. John called passivity "an offence of omission"—that its hallmark is suspended animation as the years tick by.[1] And suddenly we are out of time.

In fairy tales there are often three brothers or sisters who all receive the same invitation—often of noble birth. The first two siblings will refuse whatever the adventure is because they are already so surrounded by *stuff*. If the foray involves venturing into the forest or possibly suffering for a greater good, they refuse the call. But occasionally they may peer from the gates of the compound and wonder at this strange compulsion they may feel in their heart. Distant drums. This is passivity. Feeling the urge and not responding.

It's the third sibling who picks up the feather, talks to the farm girl, follows the breadcrumbs through the forest. They have a lovely humbleness to them. There's a forward-moving energy to them, they're not sedated by things. It may take us sixty years to get to this state in our own lives; we may have to move through a great deal of disillusion to get there, we may have to live a few seasons like the first two siblings. We—as is the case in so many stories—have to encounter the Underworld before sufficient urgency is engendered.

I once knew a man who hit collision after collision in his forties. His marriage ended and he fell into too much drinking, too much sex, too much sugar. His weight ballooned. I always saw him as driven, but, as is often the case, the stewarding of his private life was chaotic. He could be found asleep in the bath with a third of a bottle of whisky in his pint glass, belly distended with fast food, losing track of whoever tonight's "girlfriend" was. Self-medicating gone amok, he was heading somewhere terrifically dark. When doctors began to circle, the sheer passivity of his lifestyle actually shamed him into action. Occasionally shame is a very useful wake-up call.

He didn't go on vigil, or a monastic retreat, he joined a gym. Stuck a pair of headphones on and listened to *Moby Dick* as he stressed his out-of-shape body into the knowledge that a change had finally come. The gym took on a sacred quality, a feeling of hope. It wasn't just "working out"; he had a whole set of rituals that went with it. When he put on his running shoes his posture changed, he held his head up. Sometimes the muscles need to be worked just as much as the mind. When *Moby Dick* finished he moved on to *The Odyssey*, and then *The Brothers Karamazov*. His break with slumber, his awakening, came with taking charge of his health. That was his quest, his voyage, his vigil. To everyone else he was another guy wheezing on the running machine; they couldn't see the hard and magnificent yards he was undergoing. He was out there with Odysseus, he was roaming with Beowulf. He was steadfast in his desire to get healthy, and restless in his motivation to heal. He soberly saw what was necessary, and he did it. He became an adult. He centered himself, and dared to consider it quietly heroic. He allowed himself to lean back into myth.

In a Russian folktale, three brothers try and stay awake to find out who's stealing golden apples from their father's tree. The first two, surrounded by blankets and hot chocolate, don't last an hour. But the third brother sits alert in the branches of a tree to force wakefulness. The discipline of those dark hours enables him to see when the firebird sweeps by and takes the apples. From there the deep adventure begins. We do not serve our culture well when we remove the option of the night vigil. We do not honour our teacher when a church is all familiarity and fuzziness as we endlessly weave and bob with whatever today's societal mandate happens to be.

Without steadfastness we would never have the discipline for the night vigil, without restlessness we would never have the adventure that God desires for us. To be humbly in touch with both is more a transmission of truth than any apologetics we can muster.

Not surprisingly, I have a story about this, often called "The Fire-bird and the Hunter."

Once upon a time a young hunter entered a forest astride his horse. It was a powerful beast, the kind we rarely find in this world anymore. As they travelled the forest grew very quiet. At a turn in the track they came across a large feather blocking their way—as long as a swan's wing, as wide as an eagle's. It radiated a strange light, like many candles had been lit. This was a feather from the firebird herself. The hunter had never wanted anything in his life like that feather. He swung down from his horse and was about to pick it up when the horse spoke:

Don't pick up that feather. If you do, you will come to know fear and trouble.

That sobered the hunter. He trusted his horse. He tried to retrace his steps, but it was simply too painful. He decided a compromise would be to give the feather to the king.

The king was pleased with the gift, but a thought occurred to him. A real gift for a sovereign would be not a firebird's feather, but the bird itself. Giving the boy till dawn to produce the bird, the lad wandered to the stable for advice from his horse. The horse listened to his moans, observed his tears, and simply said:

Don't weep now, the trouble is before you. Ask the king for a hundred bags of grain and three cords of rope, and tell him you'll present the bird at breakfast.

A little chutzpah goes a long way in such situations.

The hunter, following the horse's advice, spread the grain all over the meadow between the castle and the forest. At dawn the firebird flew past and thought the grain was a gift laid out by the villagers. Many years before, they would have spoken words of praise as she flew past. Grain wasn't quite as enriching, but she stopped for a bite. It was then the horse emerged from one side and the hunter from the other, swinging a rope. He'd spent a long night sleeping in a hollow tree. With a hoof on one wing, the bird was easily captured. The hunter's life was saved.

The surprised king then sent the hunter out on a much more involved expedition: to locate a woman called Vasilisa, who lived across nine lands and nine oceans. The king longed to marry her, but she'd long rejected him. The hunter again went to the horse, weeping those tears for the still deepening situation. The horse spoke.

Don't weep now, the trouble is before you. This woman only cares for beautiful things made slowly by hand. She can't be bought by persuasion or threat. Gather everything of true, handmade beauty in the king's castle and we will set out.

Long was the journey to Vasilisa, maybe years in our lives. It turned out she mostly lived on a little coracle, sailing back and forth on the waves of a distant sea at the edge of the world. Finally arriving at the spot, the hunter erected a glorious tent with tapestries and rugs. He started to cook a meal, and then as it bubbled and simmered, sang old, heart-achingly wonderful songs over the bruise-coloured waves.

Well, this was enough to attract Vasilisa. She spotted the tent, smelt the food, heard the song, and wandered up the beach. They got on famously, she and the hunter. She had songs of the sea, and many jokes; he had tales of the woods and many riddles. If you'd peered in the tent doorway, you'd suspect they might rather like each other.

After a few glasses of wine and much singing, Vasilisa fell asleep by the fire. The image of the king appeared in the boy's head, threatening all sorts of torture. The hunter panicked, tied the woman up, and took her back to the king. She was a snorting horse of fury, and spoke not a word to the boy the entire journey.

When Vasilisa met the king, she looked at both him and the hunter and finally spoke. She said she would not consider marrying the king without her wedding dress, which was, of course, where she was kidnapped months before. And the only person she would contemplate fetching it was that wretched hunter. When the king tried to persuade her to have one made at the castle, she spoke:

My wedding dress has ten thousand secrets sewn into it by my mother and aunts, grannies and great-grandmothers. Do you really think I would enter a union with a man without such a dress? It abides at the bottom of the ocean, under a rock.

Well, it was another arduous journey across nine lands and nine oceans for the hunter. There could be the first flecks of silver in his beard now. When he got there he confessed to his ever-steadfast horse that he couldn't swim. Why would he? He'd only ever known the forest. Picking up the feather had taken him farther than he'd ever anticipated.

The horse sang the kind of song you only carry when you're solid to your core. An ancient murmuration of a sound that called all the nautical creatures to attend them. Led by a crab, and on the request of the horse, they indeed sunk to the depths the hunter could not achieve, pushed the rock away, and swam up with the dress of ten thousand secrets.

When, bedraggled and with even more silver in his beard, the hunter returned with the dress for Vasilisa, he prayed his part in the story was done. Holding the dress protectively close to her, Vasilisa turned to the king.

It appears our wedding hour approaches. I have one more request. Erect a large cauldron of water in the wedding hall, with a fierce fire beneath it. When the water bubbles and the cauldron itself groans with heat, I would wish you to have the hunter thrown in. That would be my wedding gift from you.

Even by the king's standards—and he was a cruel man—this was a little much. Still, he readily agreed. The hunter was allowed one last audience with his horse. In the dark of the stable the horse looked up at the hunter and said:

Weep now.

Weep now, because it is your death you are facing.

You've loved me since I was a foal, and have ridden on my back these many years. My final advice to you is how to die. Don't run from your death. Don't wait for the guards to drag you, don't look into the crowds for your loved ones. Pick up your pace and run towards the cauldron, and when you get there jump, don't be thrown.

For a minute or two the hunter and his horse put their heads together, as if they were praying in the chapel of the stable. When the hunter returned to the wedding hall, all was prepared. Like the horse commended, the hunter wasn't dragged and didn't plead, but ran the length of the hall, leapt in the air, and disappeared under the boiling water.

For twenty minutes he was not seen.

Finally, against all conceivable odds, he stood up in the swirling waters. Not only had he survived, he looked burnished in gold, he looked like a hero from one of the old stories. Vasilisa did not look entirely surprised. Once he had climbed from the cauldron the king had the idea to repeat the experiment. He himself would take to the transforming waters.

He too ran the hall, waved to his mother, and leapt in. All waited. He did not emerge, not ever. In fact, after an hour the cauldron was drained and the body of a very old man was dragged out. In the meantime Vasilisa and the hunter were in deep conversation, he explaining his nerves at their first meeting and his true feelings, then detailing the labours of obtaining the dress and the ordeal of the cauldron. Love, finally—the love that was there all along—could emerge from the shadows and into the light. Not surprisingly it was they indeed that married, and the very first thing they did was free the firebird, who flew round and round the married couple then happily out the door and up above the forest. The horse came in to watch the proceedings and munch the very freshest hay. All were approaching jubilation, or as much as it is right for us simple humans to experience.

THE HORSE AND THE FIREBIRD

The story, beloved by many storytellers, has something enormous to show us. The horse is a robust symbol of steadfastness, the firebird a lively image of restlessness. When we—as the hunter—side with one entirely over the other, we live a dangerous half-life. If we side only with the horse we never pick up the feather (and our journey to maturation never begins), but if we keep the feather for ourselves we risk such flying too near the sun and being annihilated. I once told this story with the great John Densmore of The Doors accompanying me on percussion. Later he told me he felt that Jim Morrison let go entirely of the horse and jumped on the back of the firebird: *Watching him on stage every night was like seeing a man in a microwave—he was going to get incinerated.*

So the horse gives a legitimate caution. He recognises a flamboyant, possibly dangerous energy arriving in the boy's life. It doesn't have the steady plod of hoof but the soaring excitement of a wing.

When he takes the feather to the sovereign, he's bringing it to a figure that will always want more. First the firebird, then Vasilisa. Some
Russians regard her as the soul itself, a being that can only be courted
by long, arduous journeys and gifts made by hand. So by picking up
the feather the hunter has entered the great adventure of his life. And
any adventure involves jeopardy.

But we notice he's still taking counsel from his steadfast horse.
Even though the pace of the tale is firebird fast, he hasn't broken connection with that steadying eye the horse maintains. We all groan
when he takes Vasilisa back to the king. It seems so disrespectful, so
clumsy after their starstruck meeting. Of course the lad is quaking
because of the king's threats, even as his heart thumps for Vasilisa.
However, this is what we call *the correct mistake*. Without this grievous act the boy would never end up in the pot, which is the exact
place he's meant to be! As with all initiation stories, something in
him has to die. There is the strong sense that Vasilisa knows all along
what is happening, as does the firebird. In the tapestry of the boy's
maturation—remember this all takes a long time—everyone is playing their part, even the king.

This story tells us we need connection to a steadfast horse and a
glorious feather. Something that leads us on. The story also leads us
from fire to water. The firebird's feather leads to the deep waters of
the wedding dress of ten thousand secrets. From spirit to soul; spirit
being associated with fire and eros, soul being connected with water
and psyche. There is a sense that we have entered a very ancient part
of the story with the wedding dress. That there is a deep psychic
ocean that modern people know little about, and that at the bottom
of that ocean is such a dress. It's also worth knowing that no man can
really dive in those waters. With the best will in the world, it requires an animal—or fish—ally.

When the spirit-fire heats the soul-waters of the cauldron, then finally transformative change can occur in the hunter, and Vasilisa can at last locate her true husband. It was likely this was always her story to begin with. Would that all our daughters have a wedding dress like that. So Vasilisa—who is rumoured to be thousands of years old—has a man truly grown; humbled, tested, and deepened. Together they stand at the peak of a wild mountain, twin fires.

This story and its alchemical codification tell us an enormous amount about life. To cleave to the steadfast but also to lean to the wind, to court the soul and be prepared to forgive. This is a story to be digested slowly. This is a wisdom tale to help absorb and integrate all the miles climbed. Too many of us choose one over the other, the horse or the firebird, rather than live in the low cello note of *both*. Such an endeavour makes us saltier, stranger, possibly more eccentric, and I see no great harm in that, no harm at all.

6

ON PASSION

I located passion in poetry long before I found it in the arms of a girl. As a teenager I was always talking myself out of a warm embrace by droning out another Yeats poem. This was partially blind terror at the dawning reality that the woman may actually be fond of me. This, filled with self-loathing as I was, was almost disturbing. So, on I would warble, passionately deflecting the passion that was actually, patiently, standing in front of me. It would be a long walk home that night.

In our adventure of getting made, we should make friends with passion. But making friends with passion means understanding passion, both its exalted and degraded dimensions. In my early thirties I discovered the majesty of Pablo Neruda's poems (Yeats and I were on a break). I sat outside the black tent that was my home and gazed over a robust valley of oaks. I was never penny-poorer, but rarely emotionally richer. Slowly, deeply, I learnt to memorise Neruda's luscious poems. I felt I had no choice in the matter. I longed for some of their ornate but profound dignity in my life—I still do. By learning Neruda's words by heart, I started to create a considered dialogue with what you could call the erotic dimensions of life. I don't disregard my passions or appetites, I refine them. I don't need to start a fire so large I burn the village down, I don't require so much sun I get a melanoma, I don't need to eat till I'm sick. I work with them, elevate them, but they don't own the house.

I've noticed recently a lack of new love songs on the radio. Songs that celebrate the nuance of the romantic experience, its sheer complexity of feeling. What seems to have replaced the Leonard Cohens and Joni Mitchells is an even greater dive to the nether regions. There are fewer bards about; it's all about the booty. The Troubadours said this when they discovered Moorish love poetry:

We have the bread, now we have the knife.

Some refinement has arrived. We no longer just tear the bread of the erotic with our hands, but have a blade to give it specificity and boundaries. A dance needs its steps to create its innate drama and tension. Endless rutting is terrifically unsexy. I worry the knife has long been chucked into the bushes and brutish knights are wandering the fields all over again, looking for the farmers' girls. There is enormous loss in this, and substantial danger. Sex without the refinement of passion becomes the new normal.

No sex is casual sex. I've sometimes wished it was, but I can't hang my heart on it. Or my conscience. It's not that all intimacy is meant to be lofty and serious—please no—but that it always comes with some kind of consequence. If it's perfunctory and transactional it often leaves us troubled. If it's engaging and transforming it leaves us blissed, even peaceful. There's quite the difference. One leaves us free, the other oddly bound.

It's a strange state of affairs, as if we are not quite keeping up with the emotional intelligence of our own bodies. In the massively over-stimulated, oversexed waters that we now swim in, it rarely seems that stacking up the body count (a modern and oddly telling phrase) makes us feel liberated at all. Most of us wouldn't have the capacity to make a deep connection with the polyamorous rapidity that sections of the internet encourage. We sense that this is not a liberation, but that it feels like a cheapening. Like so many, I've been down in the trenches with this reality; I'm not writing this from a hut above the cloud line.

Ironically, statistically at least, young people seem to be having less sex than before. Fewer teenage pregnancies, fewer bunk-ups in the graveyard after a few sips of vodka. There are various theories about this, but the most common theory is this: Sex can't compete with porn. For those inculcated in pornography since adolescence, the theatre and ever-darkening scenarios it offers are far safer places to inhabit than the mysterious and even sacred encounters possible with a real human being. Why chance the subtle nuances of courtship and the possibility of underperforming when you can just shuffle off with your phone into a virtual world where nothing is actually risked? It's an odd, growingly familiar combination of lust and loneliness.

As a mythologist I wonder if we are moving from red shoes to silver hands. In folklore red shoes are a sign of unbridled desire, silver hands a sign of remove from direct contact. In the fairy tale "The Handless Maiden," a young woman's hands are cut off as a result of a terrible bargain her father makes. For a period she wears silver hands before abandoning them in the slow and more difficult labour of growing her own hands back. The spectacle of hyper-porn is a silver-handed addiction. It's a strangely removed activity, despite the ever-growing intensity of its images.

Part of porn's silver-handedness is a direct compromise to our imagination. Sex is not something created between the intimacy of two people, bespoke and emerging, but mechanically laid out for the retinas. It's oddly passive. It doesn't even involve the twists and turns of your own mental conjuring. In ancient times there would have been gods and goddesses invoked for lovemaking; Aphrodite goddess of love or Dionysus god of wine, for example, but I don't believe they'd be showing up for the viewing of porn.

An old Inuit story of the same name suggests if you get your heart broken you may end up on the moon. From the moon you can watch everything that goes on down on earth, but it's no longer going to hurt you, there's little risk attached. But from that perspective nothing is going to claim you either. Again, to dwell there is a silver-handed position. The twist in the Moon Palace story is that it turns out it's only three short steps away from our world. You can in fact wander our streets but secretly, safely, lonesomely dwell in the Moon Palace.

There's an impotence to this moon-dwelling. It's a "safe space" as the modern parlance goes. But while it preserves life, it doesn't instigate life. There's a difference. There's nothing getting born up/in there. There's no risk. And that's all we're told we need these days. But humans have hardly been risk-averse creatures. At some point we have to reach out and touch the universe.

All cultures, from the beginning, have known that erotic desire is one of the most combustible elements to life, and have often created elaborate rituals and stories to help contain what often seems uncontainable. And if it remains uncontainable then some sort of bacchanalian rite or May Day frolic may be introduced to accommodate the shaking of civic limits. Sex is with us from the beginning. In Egyptian creation myths the world is created by the lovemaking of Nut and Geb, the earth being male, the sky female. Nut—also known as *she who holds a thousand souls*—is covered in stars and mounts her brother, and their sex creates Osiris, Isis, Set, and Nephthys, a fifth child, Arueris, sometimes being mentioned.

Virginity was also a state taken seriously. In myth it's often more than lack of sexual experience but a loyalty to certain interior values. The virgin in you can't be bought, persuaded, or seduced. It may be that we hold to a virginity in certain areas of our life but not in others. There could be situations that are negotiable, and other standards that are not. Protecting a virgin in many ancient pictures would be a lion or serpent, powerful creatures that represent an incubation of sexual energy. The virgin is set apart, distilled, closer to God than we are. Virgin births would have been a common motif in the time of Christ; attributed to figures like Plato or Alexander the Great, it was an understood mythological language to show how, in its very implausibility, something sacred had happened. Christian scholars have often argued that this familiarity was God's way of preparing culture for the sheer strangeness of the birth of Christ. Whether we remain apart from the erotic banquet or commingle, we are aware of enormous creative attention given to legislating sexual and romantic passion.

Within Christianity, mystics have venerated the notion of their souls as brides and Christ as the bridegroom; we only have to turn to Bernard of Clairvaux or Teresa of Avila to find ecstatic treaties of God-love overflowing from the well of chastity they are gathered around. Rather than dried-up and fearful, their very devotion engenders more imagination, and of the holiest kind, Bernard writing: "The more I contemplate God, the more God looks on me. The more I pray to him, the more he thinks of me too."[1] Teresa is believed to have said something sobering: "Christ has no body now but yours. No hands, no feet on earth but yours. Yours are the eyes through which he looks compassion on this world. Yours are the feet with which he walks to do good. Yours are the hands through which he blesses all the world. Yours are the hands, yours are the feet, yours are the eyes, you are his body. Christ has no body now on earth but yours."[2] If you—in a fashion—are the body of Christ, then are you at peace with the places you take that body and the thoughts you allow fermentation? The virgin spirit contemplates and takes seriously these things.

Back awhile, we find a rather different kind of relationship between God and human, this time for the human to act as conduit on earth for the seeding of a deity. Many are familiar with Solomon's Song of Songs, maybe less so with the third-century BC hymn of the Sumerian goddess Inanna to her beloved Dumuzi. A few lines of it go like this:

> *He made me as eager as a young moon.*
> *And when I opened my door for him,*
> *It was moonlight he saw.*
> *It was time to plough my wet earth*
> *To place his ox in my furrows*
> *The cedar sapling rises to my hips*
> *With just the thought of it.*
> *My womb loved him most of all.*
> *From my womb sprung plants,*
> *From my womb sprung grain,*
> *As I gazed on the ripeness of his fields.*[3]

This ritualized adoration of desire would then become a ceremony between a priestess and a king to ensure a decent Sumerian harvest. In their copulation the myth-world of Inanna and Dumuzi found a human footing in the bodies of the sovereign and his consort. From that channel, life erupted into the fields, valleys, and rivers. Anyone spending the briefest time in nature would witness the teeming, seething rhythm of spring into the fullness of summer, then the quiet descent into autumn and winter. To the ancient mind this told us about journeys into the Underworld, of seasonal narratives matching mythic narratives matching human narratives. This was a connected universe, and our primeval erotic appetites were part of this wider oomph of life force. In its most elevated forms, it afforded more than a little dignity.

The aphrodisiac of taboo is often tied up with desire. You can't have something, so you want it all the more. It's off limits and agonizingly tempting. Taboo was a place of interest for the Troubadours. They didn't sing of random trysts; they were always site-specific for the attentions of what was called the Far Distant Lady. This lady, often the wife of their employer, tolerated as many of these winsome hymns as she could endure. The Troubadours, in theory at least, would put forth notions that adulterous love could be the only true kind, as marriage in the upper classes was usually politically motivated. Amor was the great conqueror of Roma (societal obligation), even being the same word backwards. The poems themselves generally fall shy of describing consummation, although on the rare occasion of a female Troubadour, the Countess of Dia pushes the whole affair forward with the line "I wish you would use my body as a pillow"—no lofty metaphor there.

A great favorite of the Troubadours, the story of *Tristan and Isolde* is the tale of a young couple falling madly in love after drinking a potion meant to be consumed by King Mark and Isolde (Mark being her intended but unmet husband, Tristan being sent to collect her). A highly charged affair erupts between the kids, while Mark is duped into thinking nothing is going on. Whilst their affair is illicit, hidden, fleeting, its voltage is quite remarkable; however, when they elope and have nothing but each other, the whole thing becomes tawdry and mundane. Romantic love—in adolescent mode—thrives on absence not presence. Much of the story focuses on their love as a kind of hunt for each other; when they actually *have* each other, the energy starts to wilt. A deeper connection is required. Transgression can be overrated. This brings me to a fairy tale.

There are many versions of "The Red Shoes," but it basically tells of a young girl without much money who is entranced by a pair of red shoes she sees a princess wearing. They are so different to the heavy black shoes that everyone tramps in and out of church with. The churchgoers all seem so serious, dark eyed and weighed down. Through various kindnesses she gets a similar pair of shoes. One day, outside the church, she meets a man returning from a great war, far away. He has a long white beard and very bright eyes. He starts to play a fiddle. While others disapprove, he coos and simpers over the girl's shoes, even asking her to give him a little twirl in them, a little dance. Feeling shamed by the churchgoers and affirmed by his gaze, she starts to dance. For a while it's quite wonderful, even liberating. She twirls past the villagers, round the graves, laughing and in wild excitement. She hollers and pirouettes, with the old man playing his fiddle and making her feel witnessed the whole time. For a few minutes this is quite the spectacle, but after a while, the crowd grows bored, gathers their kids, and goes home for Sunday dinner.

Point made, the laughing girl tries to stop dancing and finds she can't. The panic grows in her eyes, exciting the old man even more. He starts to play faster and leads her out of the graveyard and onto the moors and through the woods. For many hours she splashes through streams and over hills, growing more and more crazed, more exhausted. Under a full moon she spasms and twists as the fiddling man keeps pace. The ecstasy has descended into nightmare, the passion into enchantment. Her feet are bleeding and somehow glued to the shoes.

Finally she dances into the arms of an angel who frees her from the ghastly parade and liberates her feet. The old man melts away into the trees. The angel washes her feet in a stream, and over time she recovers. She is never going to wear those big heavy black shoes the others wear, but she finds gentler, sweeter rhythms to move to. When she wants to stop, she simply sits down and takes her hand-made shoes off.

This story has several messages. One is that a church that's too leaden, that lacks curiosity or any sense of wonder, is always going to cause a reverse response, a red shoes move. A log tends to float to the surface, no matter how many times you push it underwater. Some of us have attended churches with little playfulness and plenty of judgement. There are only so many tuts, sighs, and scoldings a young soul can tolerate before those red shoes look awfully tempting. The second message of the story is the clear peril of putting on the shoes. With a rebel yell we commit to whatever the thrill is and wherever it may be taking us. It would almost display a lack of character not to do so. It likely has no particular malice to it, but suddenly we are swimming into waters with far deeper currents than we may imagine.

My early life as a musician enabled almost unlimited contact with people swept up in a red shoes life. Dancing to the tune often had you dead before thirty, and in some ghastly fashion that was seen as rather credible. Rock 'n' roll eats its young. Before I started writing this, I dug out a photograph of my first proper band—one that toured and made records. All dead, apart from me, and men that would only be in their early fifties had they survived. Chaos is fetishized, disorder iconized, and we wonder why life seems so terribly combustible. And yes, in the confused and sometimes thrilling environment there was plenty of sex, plenty of drugs, plenty of attempts at some florid form of ecstasy. In more brutal versions of the story, the girl meets not an angel but villagers, who, at her prompting, cut her feet off to stop the dance. She is now crippled but safe, being wheeled in and out of church for the rest of her life, chastened but wiser. This grotesque scenario just further exaggerates the juxtaposition of rabid licentiousness and morbid ideas of purity. There is a distinct lack of imagination in both forms of acting out.

A passion for music can harden into an addiction to applause, a passion for lovemaking can cheapen into addiction to sexual relief. From a mythic way of looking at it, an overriding addiction would be a demon. A demon being something that wants us not to be liberated, not to cleave to heaven in this life. It's a word for an energy that does not wish you well. And a very wily thing to do is to make us think we are ever freer as our addictions get an even further hold.

So what do we do? We kick the robbers out of the house.

Replacing red shoes with silver hands does not help, because it is just a shape-shifting of a passion; there's no deeper enquiry in it. To be addicted to porn is to tie yourself up in knots: It's another kind of folly to sleeping around, but it's still knot tying, there's no greater liberation in it. Another element to the silver handed is control. Real sex can be unexpected, intimate, vulnerable. Porn's going to remove the risk and heighten the safety. Somehow the animal of the body will mutiny, I'm sure of it. There are already more cases of impotence among young men than ever before, and the join-the-dots connection between all of them is heavy porn use. In the end, porn wilts, rather than inflames, desire. It deadens. May take a while to get there, may take a few stops to see where the train is heading, but that's the destination. We become less "creaturely" and more zombified.

In Greek myth, desire is sparked by Eros's arrows, which fly where they will, often at folks wildly inappropriate for us (he has a wicked side). But one day the unthinkable occurs: Eros is gazing on a young woman, Psyche, and the tip of his arrow pierces his own skin as he unwittingly strokes it. He quite literally gets a taste of his own medicine. The story of *Psyche and Eros* is a tale of Underworld suffering and final redemption. *Psyche* is an old word for "soul," and Eros has always been seen as synonymous with spirit. In myth, as we know, spirit and soul don't quite do the same things. An excess of spirit in your love life can keep you eternally restless, promiscuous, always peeking over the next hill. An excess of soul will risk profound inwardness and the lurking shape of abiding depression. However, the marriage of both—after all sorts of maturities engendered as initiations—creates something quite wonderful on Mount Olympus. That marriage within *us*, containing the vitality and playfulness of Eros, and the fidelity and depth of Psyche—well, that's something to aim for. Eros has spontaneity, none of that black shoe rigidity, but Psyche has the quality of anchoring that makes a courtship into a wedding, and a wedding into a marriage. Myth shows us very useful things about the passions, and by naming them as characters in stories gives them greater clarity. Christ then lifts this all up into higher ideals—ideals that don't just work within the murk of the passions, telling us that to step beyond their negative aspects is to dwell in the biggest story of all.

It bears repeating: The body, sex, celebration, feasting, these are wonderful things given to us by a God that seems to have a big soft spot for beauty. They are aspects of a vaster journey; they are boons and blessings but not the final object of our adoration. For every feast there is the lean education of the fast. There is a relationship to all these gifts that is adult, not adolescent. Erik Varden's wonderful phrase "reconciliation of the senses" means to live free of black shoes, red shoes, and silver hands.[4] These stories are technologies for defeating demons.

ROMANTICISM COME OF AGE

The figure of the knight is often key in myths of Romanticism. Within the tradition such a knight is expected to be gracious, humble, brave, and unwavering in his discipline. They are not to remind us of their achievements. They protect those in need. At this point it's easy for our eyes to grow misty as we half remember tales of Camelot, of spires and tournaments and toasts, of midnight meetings with a lover in the orchard.

But I don't want to start there. I want to begin with something that has the scent of the Underworld about it, a murkier dimension. Something that evokes what the poet Lorca called *Duende.*[5] Because there's a deeper darkness in these stories than is maybe first apparent. For a knight there's a price sometimes referred to. Let's begin with a story from an old medieval ballad, "King Henry."[6]

> *Never should a man go wooing*
> *Who lacks these things three:*
> *A stack of gold, a kindly way*
> *And a heart of charity.*

It was late when the young king arrived at the ruins of the old hall. All day he'd been tracking a buck and found himself lost in the woods with a wild night settling around him. In what would have been the kitchen he made himself a fire and sheltered from the worst of the rain. It got darker and darker till the rain stopped, and then it got quieter and quieter.

From the deepest shadows came an old woman's voice:

> *Some meat, some meat King Henry,*
> *Bring some meat to me,*
> *Go kill your horse King Henry,*
> *And bring him here to me.*

Henry's hounds growled and pressed in against their master's boots. In the gloom the young king could just make out a pale figure, with a vast dark mouth and teeth like iron spikes.

> *Oh bring me now your berry brown horse,*
> *Oh bring your trusted steed,*
> *Oh bring me now your berry brown horse,*
> *His flesh is what I need.*

With a grieving heart he slew his own horse for the hunger of the ancient being. She gobbled it up to the fur and bones as he, horrified, watched.

> *Some meat, some meat King Henry,*
> *Bring some meat to me,*
> *Go kill your hounds King Henry,*
> *And bring them here to me.*

With a sore heart he slew his own hounds and presented them to the old one. Again, she gobbled them up to the fur and bones as he watched.

Some meat, some meat King Henry,
Bring some meat to me,
Go kill your hawk King Henry,
And bring him here to me.

With a battered heart he called his hawk down from the rafters and killed it. The one with spikes for teeth ate it.

Finally she seemed full. She crooned through the dark.

A bed of heather King Henry,
Please make a bed for me,
A bed of heather King Henry,
I wish to lie with thee.

Henry gathered the heather, made the bed, and she got in, beckoning to him.

Through the dark crawled Henry, reaching out to her cold blue shape as he leant in for the kiss she requested. As he kissed he found himself embracing a young woman, flesh and blood, the kind he'd meet in any market square in old England. Transformed, she snuggled in.

But as he felt her swollen belly pressed against him, under her taut skin he could feel his horse, his hounds, his hawk. He'd given her everything he loved.

And there, in the dark and the rain,
Henry realised exactly what it would take to be a king.

This medieval story, collected in the Child ballads, is what they call a Loathly Lady story. In the tradition, any sovereign of old England had to marry the land, and often in a most unpalatable guise. Their willingness to do this actually is what marks them as king. It's interesting to note that it's not the easy sell of a Rapunzel bride that denotes chivalric class, but a willingness to be joined to something testy, something hungry, something dark.

This is a very strange story to exist under the title of a "romance," but exist it does. And there's a whole genre of them. There's not much of a warm, cosy glow about it. The honeymoon doesn't begin for the king until—as the poets say—he's been willing to eat some darkness.

King Henry's willingness to feed an old woman, even a spectral one, is not based just on fear but on the concept of *noblesse oblige*. If you are going to be noble, you have to act noble. In other words, the courtly code has some grit in its saddlebags, it's not just floating around meadows, sipping wine, and parading macho in tournaments. A king's mettle is discerned in the middle of the night when they are lost and alone. Henry could have leapt up and struck the old woman's head off, but he's trained not to do so. His sacrifice reveals his class.

The king acts as the servant. *The first shall be last and the last shall be first.*

Despite valiant efforts, we have inherited an adolescent form of Romanticism, the reason being that as a culture we are generally frozen there: perpetually teenage and with maxed-out minds, stressed-out souls. Romantic love in full power is an *initiatory* experience. For many it's the nearest they get to a religious experience. For a time, everything seems different, elevated, magical.

These days initiations are usually accidental, not formal, rarely given the dignity of community attention. And that attention is not a vanity, it's essential for such experiences growing-us-up. We are meant to be witnessed. Certain experiences need to be exteriorised, ritualised, to help us witness quite what has changed in us. Otherwise we can stay as children for the longest time. So as our culture gets growingly more secular, our readings of these tales get growingly less nuanced, less imaginative, more teenage. Modern people simply don't understand the stories as we used to. I think our bait used to go deeper.

The adolescent mode of Romanticism doesn't seem to be available for a second act. Everything peaks at twenty-eight. You've probably noticed that this model doesn't create the greatest grown-ups. So we sober up. We replace these stories with heavy sighs, realistic goals, and insurance policies. We marry Mark or Isolde Number Two. Middle age. Just around the time we realise we can't get it up anymore. Coincidence? There has to be a third way.

I want to remind us of that earlier ballad of King Henry, or the grief cry of Antonio Machado, "What have you done with the Garden that was entrusted to you?"[7] A romanticism come of age insists we kiss the crone, or the frog, or bend from our horse to listen to the wisdom of the dwarf when we are lost in the forest.

Sometimes first loves are not just to do with being heartbroken but heart-*opened*; they are about encounters of soul too devastating to fit comfortably with our previous, settled life. They are a glimpse of the Otherworld. But to *grow* with romantic love—what C. S. Lewis called the spark that starts the engine of loving—is going to involve changes of gear, long silences, giving up addiction to permanent excitement, welcoming limit on occasion (sorry all you polyamory types).[8] I believe it's still possible to hang around the lovers tree but with a bit of weight to you, some grit in the oyster, experience of the Underworld.

And to give up the thrill of the orchard completely? *Try to be serious*. That's very uncreative, but it's not surprising people do. Porn isn't going to break your heart, love is.

Anyone who's lived a bit will have an aversion to heartbreak. The degree of loss it can provoke can take years to live through. You aren't done till you're done. Or heartbreak is done with you. And that's going to change you along the way. All sorts of self-sufficiency, trauma responses, and intimacy-avoidance issues are likely to get installed as the psyche struggles to come to terms with long-lasting and unchanging loss.

In Irish myth there is often a scent of perennial sadness, even at a high table feast. An image I have used to illustrate this over the years is this: Next to every lover's chamber there is a room filled entirely with crow feathers, and at some point in the journey of love one of you will have to go and lie down in those feathers. It is the very price tag of love, the sheer risk of it all, that dictates it. It is the other side of the coin. For such reward must also be such sweet sorrow. It could be a bereavement, divorce, or breakup, but almost no one is unmarked by it.

Loss is ungainly, and won't easily smarten up to make the rest of your life appear cool and groovy. There's zero cool and groovy about loss. There are millions of us strolling around with active loins but lock and key round our hearts. I have caused my own catalogue of disasters acting like this, and I'm ashamed of it. I was very small. And I was small because I was broken in on myself, and I was broken in on myself because I was obliterated by loss. I just didn't look like it. Still had a cheery grin pasted on.

Loss changes how food tastes, how mountains and fields look; it changes the sounds of words people say to us, muffles them, sours them. It distances us. We drift away from the pain until we are snapped back. We just don't know what to do with it until eventually we have little choice but to accommodate it. It diminishes, creates listlessness on every side, pushes us towards too much numbed sleep, hopeless shrugs, and big old cries that seem to never stop. The body just has to do what it does. We gain weight, lose weight, drink too much, yawn constantly, stare blankly. Rinse, repeat.

I once cried most days for six months. It was like throwing up. Ugly crying. By the end I had salt lines on my cheeks like I'd been eyeballing a desert wind. But you can't be a storyteller if you haven't been through something like this; you simply won't be believed. And funnily enough, though folks may claim a myth is "made up," a real storyteller will make you believe them utterly. Truth in every word.

Accommodating loss, with all its ungainly consequence, is part of being a real human.

To a Romantic it is not just what occurs in life's caravan, but how you react to it, what it makes of you. Ted Hughes touches on this in the essay "Crow on the Beach": "It is like the difference between two laughters: one bitter and destructive, the other defiant and creative, attending to what seems to be the same calamity."[9] It's what I've often called the difference between seeing and beholding.

Knowing myths and how they align with our own experience can help us emerge from loss (I'm not suggesting we ever quite leave it behind) not bitter but creative. They become a vessel for the catastrophic heaviness you may be experiencing. The stories are bigger than us. Somehow—I've done this a hundred times—I let the story carry some of the sorrow I am not quite ready to shoulder. And then telling it orally allows the sadness to take a communicable form that shifts it a little, makes it useful. It's not a magic trick, but it has slow road healing in it.

There are lovely lines in the Bible about loss that when I'm in a sympathetic mood I half believe. Sometimes there's almost nothing anyone at all can say about it to me. But I know two things. First, pray to something bigger than you. Eyeball God. Especially when you are falling asleep and are not at your most sensible. Just let it out—it doesn't have to make sense, he understands perfectly. Burble away. Lean into divine ground. I wish I'd copped on to that earlier. It'll do you far more good than a dating website. Second, to repeat, time is eventually your ally. You will not remain in quite the same place with your loss, even as you have no real choice but to accommodate it.

Don't give up love, but don't be naïve to it.

Kierkegaard wrote about three types of love. The basest was one of seduction: the addiction to pleasure and the practice of the gigolo floating from flower to flower. The second was what is found in a marriage worthy of the name—committed to each other but not as a defence against the wilder shores of romantic love; rather, something that channelled and deepened the experience, creating a door to the third and highest form: when we encounter divine ground and an experience of God. Kierkegaard names this as an experience in which "the Ego plunges through its own transparency to meet the power that created it."[10] We encounter here a radically different charge to a marriage than to the perception of the Troubadours, where such arrangements seem riven only with grinding protocol and heavy sighs.

Each generation has to figure out what romantic love is. "Love needs reinventing," as Rimbaud said, and so it does, over and over.[11] I will tell *Tristan and Isolde* as a deep and masterful story, but not as the end of the matter. From a youthful perspective love of that voltage is *always* going to lead to a kind of death; it will always burn the world around it down. Nothing can live up to it.

But once we've died a few times for love, what then? We may have a limp but we're still here, peering around in the pew. Love can't be "managed," can't be climbed, can't be subdued—not really. If it can it's not love in the way I'm thinking about.

I said a few years ago that the best poems are written not by the one that got the kiss but the one that didn't. That's kind of true but kind of bleak. And it gets less charming when you see old age not that far away. Growing older alone.

Myth is a language of hyperbole; a gestural, essential proclamation on the business of living. It's not tidy but provocative, exhaustive not clipped. It's a jumble and a jungle, a loving swoon in the face of inky black night. Myth carries our dead with us, elegantly, as our caravan swishes down the centuries. Myth is endless *epistrophe*—a turning about, seemingly concerning the past but not much to do with old times at all. I tell ancient stories because I think they are in the future too.

What I've been doing these last pages is presenting a historic movement (Romanticism) as a link between the archaic rumblings of myth and the immediate concerns of your own life. You could call it connective tissue. Much of what the poets were wrestling with we instantly identify with—it's why we remember them.

Where do you find pressure points of association? Be specific. Specificity is your friend. Buy an anthology of poems and a decent pen. When you find a line you love, underline it, and most importantly, memorise it. It will do something different in your mouth to what it does on the page. Something is being mirrored back to you. Take it seriously. A poem or a story is a teacher. They are patiently waiting. It is a wonderful thing to have a secret instructor.

In a desperate time in my own life I lived in a men's hostel above a garage where cars got pulled apart all day long. I occupied a locked room with a grubby shared bathroom. I lived on noodles and the occasional apple. But mercy of mercies, I found Twickenham Library. From there I located the key to turn my prison cell into a hermit's hut. It was there I found the bubbling brook of Dylan Thomas's words. It was there I was bundled into Russian carriages galloping through boreal forests. It was there I felt the lurch of green Aegean waves under my argonaut ship. It was in that most pitiful of circumstances I discovered the nobility of Romanticism and began to wend my way back to the myths. In a fairy tale, when you get lost in the forest, breadcrumbs diligently followed will get you out. To comb a poem, to turn a story lovingly around in your mouth, to walk the same stretch of river repeatedly—these things have dignity and information attached.

If you let them, they will deepen you.

7

ON PRAYER

I once knew an assassin. He was a student of mine. He'd gone on to, as they say, do "other things," but his earlier job stayed with him. He seemed concerned about his past actions and wanted to start the process of at least talking about it—even if he was not quite able to immediately atone for it. His own family had abandoned him. Knowing this was outside of my experience, I asked him if he'd prayed about it. He told me prayer didn't feel real to him. I asked him what did.

Money.

So I suggested he rip up a fifty-pound note every time he made a prayer, so soon it may feel significant. Not that this was God-bribery or lobbying, but it freighted the encounter with more consequence than usual. Soon enough the muddied track we were walking along was littered with torn-up pound notes. He sat by a river and was quiet. Later that night, just before midnight, his long-estranged mother rang him out of the blue after many years of silence.

There once was a man who went to temple and prayed every day.

Oh lord, please let me win the lottery.

Next day he was as broke as before. Every day he made the same prayer at temple.

Oh lord, please let me win the lottery.

After two weeks of this, a voice boomed from the heavens:

Jacob, for God's sake, buy a ticket!

I love that little story.

God can achieve all sorts of things, but we too must do our part. It's a collaborative enterprise, praying. It's not passive, though it involves surrender. The story of the assassin and his prayer has always stayed with me. I never asked him what he prayed for, but the response was profoundly and most deeply what he needed.

It's always the vulnerability that strikes me with prayer. The closing of my eyes, the shifting of weight onto my knees, the defencelessness of that moment. I am a little bird peering up from the nest. I don't feel heroic but diminished, and accommodating some usually disguised fragility. I feel my appropriate shape in the universe. This isn't a moment of accomplishment, rather sending a voice to the presence that enables me life. The notion that anyone would be listening is absolutely extraordinary. And we have made this outrageous presumption for thousands of years.

There's an antique belief that to pray is to sail out into a pregnant darkness where we will encounter God. That a prayer is as mighty as a Sinai or Tabor, as deep as the Sea of Galilee. It's that notion that causes the ancient man in me to lean forward. Much of my life he's not convinced by. This weathered old one is happiest out in the roaring forties with the Ancient of Days. He's enjoyed enough of land-life. The impulse for prayer is, of course, hardly restricted to the remit of organised religion, and my thought of what constitutes a prayer may be very different to yours.

Honestly, my prayers have sometimes been a gabble. Booted along by occasional terrors or a shopping list of want or a fumbling recital of various friends I'd wish protection over—when I remember to ask. With my prayers, I would usually sail to nowhere, ascend nowhere. They were mostly just keeping my neurosis company—toddler prayers, I suppose. Other than the Lord's Prayer—so combed over it went down with no thought at all—I would have been suspicious of any set prayers, because it was interfering with my personal freedom, man.

I don't think I respected prayers or people that prayed. It seemed beige and a bit exhausted. It was something folks did when they'd rather given up. I would smile pityingly as they said they would pray for little old me. Hah. I was out there in the world, being dramatic, making moves, baby. *They* were the ones who needed a prayer. I would pat their heads and tell them to meditate. Oh dear.

I knew crisis prayers would have more vim attached—*no atheist in a foxhole.* The kind of fervour that arises from drama, that tends to be what we associate with "real prayer." That's what I would have re- garded as prayer that lights up God's switchboard. And maybe it would. There are miraculous examples, but there are also cases where nothing much seems to happen at all. Think of the courage of "thy will be done" when you're crucified in the Underworld of your terror. Well, it's ghastly. Prayer never feels more real than at those moments.

Prayer comes from the Old French *prier,* which actually means "to request," so maybe the shopping list notion isn't that recent. It's often connected with a robust desire to *stay alive.* We pray to petition our fate. But over the years I've been around a fair few approaches: I've seen Sufis swaying, I've sat in the smoke of the midnight longhouse as First Nations folks danced their prayers, I've seen Christians speak in languages I don't understand with their arms extended, I've sat quietly with the Quakers, rarely a peep from them. Sometimes prayers seem about making an interior contact, at other times wildly extro-verted, and many gradients between the two. It can be alarmingly casual or distressingly ornate. It has bells and smells, it has no bells and smells, it's taking place in remote chapels, it's happening on the dance floor, you can take your pick.

What would seem to unite the encounters and the accoutrements is focus on what's been called "vertical attention": We are stretching ourselves through word and movement to contact John Moriarty's "divine ground."[1] It's not just personal display we are after, but some kind of return message. We are looking to connect with the source.

A prayer shouldn't be a spell, though magic in the most redemp-tive sense should be present. Not magic as a bending of existence to your will, but magic as the capacity for wonder and trust in a God that can do all. "We are because he is," reminds Rowan Williams.[2] He loves us, wants to hear from us, and we don't have to go round the houses to get his attention.

Prayers degenerate into grubby formulas when they are cosmi-cally on the take; they are raised to spiritual poetry when they have blessing and gratitude at their core. But to relegate magic entirely from praying is to shoot the bird out of the sky. When I attend Di-vine Liturgy I am altered the moment I walk through the door. In the darkness I light candles for the dead, kiss icons, prostrate on the stone floor, chant or sing prayers and scripture over and over, imbibe sacred incense, stay standing sometimes in discomfort whilst already weakened by fast. And then, at the height of the ceremony, we eat our God. Sounds pretty magical to me. When I emerge at the end, I am in no doubt whatsoever that something has just happened.

I love the physicality of the encounter, the engagement of the senses, the fleshly embodiment of the ceremony. In the words of Philip and Carol Zaleski in their book *Prayer: A History*:

It was necessary and inevitable, and not a matter for Christians to regret, that the magic of the gospel would partake of the magic of the ancient world and would commingle with the folk magic of many cultures to which Christianity spread. The relics, rosary beads, statues, icons, medals, and votive offerings that line the old highways of Europe, and especially the pilgrimage routes; the magical uses of familial prayers; the vigils, pilgrimages, processions, novenas, and litanies of the faithful— all these are signs not of atavism or degeneration, but rather of a fully realised culture of prayer.[3]

But there are differences between old and new. Plenty. To the early Christians prayer was not a loquacious recital like it was for their neighbours the pagans, but rather an impassioned plea, a loving of their enemy, a call to be emboldened to spread the good news, to wish courage to not just their immediate community but all over the Mediterranean. After the martyrdom of both Peter and Paul, public preaching briefly tailed off, though it continued in the houses of believers. Prayer, however, was everywhere. The immediacy of the prayers mirrored the perception of a God who had heart for their suffering and was attending to their speech.

Over time these early believers came to develop a hardy patience for a response to their prayers, as well as the occasional lightning-quick development. As the scholar Alan Kreider reminds us, part of prayer's attraction in those communities was that it helped them cope.[4] Life was often short, uncertain, and persecution loomed: You would want to be communing regularly with God. It stabilised as the world lurched. And personal reconciliation was central: You were not to leave a quibble unattended before praying; you were to get right with your neighbour for the greater spiritual good. Such prayer ennobled the Christian to live with more confidence, to have more surety in their actions. It seems that the attraction of the early communities was not through rabid evangelising but a lifestyle that was uncommon and rather fearless. Prayer was central to this confidence.

Yeshua uses prayer as nothing less than spiritual combat with the Luciferic: "This kind cannot be driven out by anything but prayer," he says.[5] He is rarely more direct than at these moments. The force of his words turns crisis to rapture. He's not cloaked in recital or obscuration; he simply couldn't be clearer. His prayers have instant results, and he encourages us to believe ours can achieve the same. There's nothing wistful or opaque in his spiritual technologies. In a time of catastrophic import, at Gethsemane he falls to the ground as he prays—"Let this cup pass from me"—and in the next breath asks only for his Father's will to happen.[6] He prays for those often confused and competitive companions, his disciples; he prays that we love ones who aim their malice towards us; he prays continually and does his worship early in the morning, out in the groves of wild solitude.

John Chrysostom wrote that prayer acts as a harbour for those blown by the storm, is a staff for the weak-limbed, an anchor for the shipwreck, a treasury for the poor.[7] It was considered access to pleasure, an experience of joy, and a practice that gave horror to demons. From his view, no Christian should be anything but delighted to swim in those luxuriant waters of devotion. Prayer is a form of self-regulating where we grow in consciousness of our true nature. Prayer is not static but dynamic, even within liturgical repetitions. We are in movement, falling yet deeper into the mind of God. Prayer lubricates our acts of charity, gifting poetic resonance to the small coursecorrectives needed for a day trying to live in the wonderful trouble of the Christ-light.

In the Divine Liturgy it is perceived the saints are even closer than usual. As prayers were sung, St. John of Kronstadt would claim that he could hear Moses and Zacharias singing, even Mary on occasion.[8] Our prayers are wafted aloft by holy ancestors. In the Eastern mind all the saints are gathered with Christ, everyone happily gathered within his wider body. It's lively and bustling, even when we ourselves may be praying alone in a bedsit or moonlit hill. We are actually buoyed and surrounded. Such prayer overcomes the notion of an abyss between humans and God. Such an abyss would be a hell-state. And to overcome such a thing would be to give the prayer an address, and that address would be Christ.

The Irishman John Moriarty was a sometimes philosopher, sometimes gardener, sometimes storyteller with an extraordinary way of looking at the world. As I think about prayer, I'm thinking about a story he used to tell, the story of Big Mike. Big Mike returns to the cottage of his childhood on a remote island. Over time he is reintroduced to his neighbours and starts to fish with the men. After a time, he goes out alone, and far from the shore. This is terrifying behaviour, and hard to fathom. The settlement gradually realises he's out there in the carnivorous depths with no nets. What on earth, what in God's name is he doing? Finally, to his friend Ned he explains the nature of his doings:

> Night after night, I cast the net of my mind into the ocean of experience. Into it also I cast the net of my heart. Every morning, hauling the net of my mind, I hoped that in it I would find the great creed, the great knowing. But I never did. Neither did I, hauling the net of my heart, find it in the great emotion, the great saving passion or rapture. In both nets, from time to time, I found marvels. But I didn't find final healing.

Final healing isn't healing of the mind, nor is it healing of the heart. It is healing beyond them, into Divine Ground. Divine Ground within. Divine Ground below passion and love in the human heart, below knowing in the human mind.

I rowed myself out, and it's true Ned, it's true.

Out there, in that Divine Dark,

Out there, in that Divine Deep,

The fishing, not fishing at all,

Is blessedness, is bliss.[9]

In Orthodoxy we would call that meeting the Uncreated Light. And a way to get there is through Hesychasm. Hesychasm is a very deep form of stillness, often aided by a version of the Jesus prayer:

Lord Jesus Christ, Son of God, have mercy on me.

Though repeated, it's not a mantra, it's not a spell, but an act of extremely beautiful contrition. It's powerful. Powerful beyond pronouncements of self-loathing and masochistic admonishments. It is a settling of your knees into the millennia-weathered grooves of other pilgrims' prostrations. It is a taking of that proper shape I mentioned. There's not much to ask for at that moment, so deep is the experience announcing itself.

A wilderness idea from a Christian source is that this is only possible when the mind is nested within the terrain of the heart. What could that mean? There would be any number of ways to describe such a thing, and all of them would fall grievously short. My own small experience has been like this: I sit in a darkened room and am still for a few minutes. When my breathing has naturally slowed, I repeat the prayer. Each turn of the words is a universe within itself; the words have the pregnancy of space between repetitions and are not blurted rapid-fire. I'm not trying to ramp anything up. I don't visualise anything, religious or otherwise. I do pay attention to what I'm saying. After about ten minutes there is the distinct sensation that the prayer is now being repeated even in my silence, like the turning of a mill wheel. And yes, abstract as it may sound, it feels as if that prayer is issuing from what I can only call the heart.

For me the heart is a place that feels both wholesome and immeasurably deep. This Christian kind of heart at least. What we could call the Romantic heart is often a more conflicted terrain. The Christian heart at best feels combed through, receptive, quiet, patient, denuded of urgency. The prayer rests there, like a pulse. Any wishes I may have, God already knows about, and the urge to petition at such a moment is absolutely redundant. For a while, I am in the Garden, or as near as a human can be.

This kind of terrain would not be regarded as the exclusive territory of monks, but a ground of orientation available to all Orthodox Christians. But our monks are less distracted than we are, more athletic in their focus, more acute in their theosis. In this way they point towards the best in us. In this way they are the most profoundly human of us. Human in a fashion that points towards Edenic design.

A hermit may ask a visitor:

Do you come from the world?

I do.

How is it out there?

Praying from this hermit place is not worldly praying, not secular wish-listing, but a reorientation to absolute poverty of spirit. That takes a moment to understand. Poverty in the sense of clinging to nothing that rinky-dink society dangles in front of us, but a mighty, lionlike poverty that moves mountains. Poverty is an upside-down, Christ-side-up form of strength. An eye-of-the-needle-ness strength. Riches abide, but not the ones we're meant to be castrating our every waking hour to achieve. Humility of soul. Persian poets say at some point we all must walk naked on the road. It's the only sane thing to do. It's how you spot a human being. A hermit would be a valuable energy for us to contemplate; not some crabby old soul who gripes at daylight, but someone who has sat in the shuddering crucible of prayer and been cooked by it, changed by it. Someone wizened and friendly with solitude. We should be paying more attention to our elders.

I would say yes to a prayer that reaches out over the companionable objects of our day, yes to prayers for more charity, resilience, good-naturedness, and also a listening kind of praying that is tucked somewhere always in our heart, mystically turning to ever greater reality. What a woeful thing it would be to be denied prayer, to be numbed to its gratitude. We can live without a great deal, but to live entirely without prayer would leave us lesser human beings. Prayer changes our relationships with pretty much everything. In the tribulation of night I turn the wheel of my prayer rope and steer my ship over woeful seas. In the brightness of a longed-for dawn I stare east and am deep-rooted in the wallop of my amazement.

In the end, prayer isn't something we do; it becomes something that we are.

As a child when I watched people praying, I sometimes saw them make the sign of the cross. I have to confess, it sometimes looked more like a warding off than an opening up. Like deflecting a vampire or a speeding ticket. *Let it not be so,* or *Please help me.* It seemed to defend or keep at bay, rather than enfold and celebrate. It seemed possibly neurotic. Whilst I have a radically different relationship to it now, it's better to be honest about my initial response. It seemed a nervous tic in a grizzly world.

It was reading the old Celtic tale of the voyage of Brendan that got me thinking again about the Signum Crucis—the sign of the cross. In St. Brendan's journey to the Hidden Country (America) it proved to be no straight line, but a circling between three points. One was the whale Jasconius, a second was a tree filled with singing birds, and the third was an abbey of silent monastics. Getting to where you longed to be required familiarity with a whale-deep consciousness, a birdlike elevation, and the broad, warm textures of profound silence. An underworld, an upper world, and a middle world. I love this. There's a religious map, right there.

I started to think of how Brendan would cross himself, or St. Brigid. Brain, shoulders, and belly wouldn't be enough. A Crossing (*literally* between mundane and sacred space) that was big enough for the world's tears and the earth's joy. Moriarty spoke about this more than once. St. Francis lived this. St. Kevin took shape so long a bird nested in his palm. A Crossing that proved an ecology of genuflection.

Maybe we are in crisis, and the more perfunctory Crossing shows us that. To be fair, I'm not unsympathetic. We do need a crash helmet half the time. Much of what gets flung at us can seem more spell than prayer, more curse than blessing. Not surprising the body starts to stiffen and tense; and my Signum Crucis can seem more like a breastplate into battle than a gathering in of the million-precious-things. It can feel there's an evil eye about, and that makes us neurotic (which can be an oddly addictive state). But I don't want to scuttle about like that, from shadow to shadow. There's no generosity in that: I'm not celebrating a miracle but watching my back. So what would I be reclaiming? Have I lost so much innocence I can no longer convincingly cast-the-gesture? (If you are losing track slightly—I'm referring to my own awareness as I make the cross, rather than the exterior action.)

Could the innocence lost be freighted with the experience gained?

Could the Crossing have more weight when nested in the absence of a childlike original participation? That the struggle is worth something, in all its Fall-ian tendrils. That it's a grown-up making the Crossing.

A Signum Crucis as: *an earth-shaped discernment of grace.*

The big sweep, the love gesture. A meeting with Heavenly Earth. Within it would be far distant mountains, toucan feathers, antelope tracks. Within it would be a thousand bad decisions fessed up. Within it would be fur and wing, star and sea. Within it would be homeless shelters, food banks, and the desperately lost, the desperately lonely.

I'm a big guy, and when I genuflect—get on one knee—my world shakes a little. And that's how it should be. It reduces me, settles me, humbles me. It's healthy.

A lot of what is wrong spiritually is feeling endlessly defensive. That sends out the wrong scent. A Crossing should literally be a *crossing-over* into mythic ground. An attention that makes the daily luminous. We all have our ways, or should figure them. I'm not really talking about a change of ceremony but a deepening of heart, and maybe that itself is the ritual. That when we make the sign of the cross, gathered within it is all precious things, healed or in need of healing. Not some perfunctory gesture for our own gain, but a warm stabling for all.

A final story:

You will remember the assassin from the beginning of the chapter and his cash-ripping prayers. Over the next few years I would offer this cash-ripping endeavour wherever I went teaching abroad. I became the cash-ripping guy. It proved oddly refreshing for everybody. I would always gather up the floaty bits and bury them when I returned to England. At the end of a long trip I found myself in Providence, Rhode Island. I was suddenly pulled out of the line for a bag inspection. I knew that there were several thousand dollars in ripped-up notes on top of my clothes. This was not going to be good. This was going to lead to further, deeper, more forensic questioning. The impassive inspections officer seemed bored but insistent to see inside my bag.

Now it was my time to pray. I shot up a fervent request that some kind of Jedi mind trick would take place and he just wouldn't see the endless, baffling, ripped-up notes.

PPPPlease Lord. I know it's been a really, really long time.

The officer carried the bag onto a separate counter and unzipped. It seemed those dollars had even multiplied since I packed the bag. It was literally *all* I could see, or that he could see, I imagine. He stared, then looked at me, then stared again, at the hundreds of ripped-up notes.

He was silent for what seemed like a minute. He grunted and shifted his weight. He zipped the bag up and handed it back to me.

I'm not even going to ask.

8

ON GUILT

There was once a young monk carrying the body of Christ across Ireland. As he crossed a meadow there was suddenly a cloud of bees surrounding him, and he fell to his knees. It wasn't an unpleasant, rather mystical experience. But one way or another he swooned unconscious into the grass, and when he woke the body of Christ was gone. As a horrible flush of guilt and shame set about him, he berated himself: *You only had one job, one job!*

So horrified was he, he spoke of it to no one. But that just cranked the guilt up even worse. For one whole year he suffered like this, until finally, exhausted, he confessed all in prayer. Immediately an angel appeared, with startling news.

You poor lad. You mean to tell me you've been suffering like this for a whole year? It had been decided that the body of Christ was to spend some time with the bees, not just the bishops. The arrival of the bees was the perfect, allotted moment. We really should have told you. Anyway, from now on, your job is to bring people to the bee chapel where they lead bee communions to our Lord every day.

Thrilled, and suddenly lighter, the monk was led by the angel to the very bee chapel where he did indeed start his new job as a guide. Over his life, thousands of folk were delighted to be brought into the presence of Christ and the bees.

I love this little story, and I always ask my students this question afterwards:

When has honey been made from what you regarded as a failure?

We don't always see the bigger picture in the moment, and can create all sorts of torture for ourselves in the short term. I remember being like that monk as a young boy, carrying around all sorts of shameful, supposedly guilty secrets that tormented me. I would throw away stories as swiftly as a bird moults and dwell in endless partial fictions. I would have had little facility to confess. Life in its ornery and mystical passage often shines a more profound light further down the line. Even so, it's not hard to live in a sepia-tinged world of regret if we allow ourselves, and having no sense of sin at all is hardly an enlightened state. Myths make some emphasis on the ability to endure a certain amount of paradox, and this can help us slowly gain a more nuanced footing in the realm of guilt. Let me tell you another story about Ireland, this one much more recent.

It's 6 a.m. in Dublin. Already light since 4. I'd wandered the town the night before for lamb kebab and a guzzle of wine before crawling into bed, and was then serenaded by a thousand Dubs singing "Wonderwall" by Oasis, apparently directly under my window. Well, finally the fledgling bards rest, and I'm waiting for my ride by the Liffey. A taxi man strides across the tarmac to meet me. Big lad, skin the colour of good bacon. A lot of energy for so early in the morning, seventies I would guess.

I still have the bitter taste of instant coffee from the hotel in my mouth and shuffle zombified into the back seat. We pass through the familiar streets of James Joyce, Ronnie Drew, Sinéad O'Connor, Phil Lynott. I'm expecting silence. He hears I'm British.

Terrible thing you did to us. Terrible.

Pardon?

With the potatoes. That was awful of you.

Not "the English," or "the Empire," but *you.* He's talking about the famine, and I'm on trial. It's oddly refreshing. There's a spotlight on me and he's expecting a response. His green eyes are drilling down into me from the driver's mirror. *How do you live with it?* I thought it was a great question; the challenge was which part of me was to respond. The acceptable thing to do would be to shudder into a quite natural contrition, to grumpily heft the nineteenth-century Irish potato famine onto my born-in-1971 shoulders. *The Hunger* they call it.

A horrible, eviscerating thing, the consequence of which is writ large in all sorts of elements of Irish life. It could be a religious act to take on its enormity, to accept the dark grandiosity of the taxi driver's singularity of questioning. To gobble the sin of it. *It was me and only me that did this to Ireland.*

I would confess all, get the cab to pull over, and run mad through the streets, then barefoot through the open fields, barking mad as Sweeney till I get to Brú na Bóinne, where a priest with spiral tattoos and a pale knife would cut my wicked heart from my chest. Take what was inside and make it outside, expose my throb-throb-throb to the soft rain and the assembled tribe. *Lads, we may be out of potatoes, but we've got this fecker's heart.*

So I could have fallen grovelling onto the plastic floor of the taxi and suggested something like that. That would have been all right, I think. All of that, in about a second and a half, came to mind.

But the other response was this: I have something to do with it, but not at all in the way you expect.

It's that very same starvation that would have had people of mine leaving Ireland themselves, making the trip to Liverpool or Manchester or London. I am one who left, talking to you who stayed. Who left Mayo, Connemara, Kerry. Who got their senses rearranged by living with the enemy-across-the-water for a hundred and seventy years. Marrying in, shifting dialect, learning new professions, getting battered for an Irish lilt, feeling guilt as their guts finally swelled with a good meal, leathering into some of those precious potatoes. I could speak as an exiled partial-Irish, trying to come home. If you pull the lens out for a moment, over only several generations, that's a legitimate voice.

So the taxi is no longer a taxi, but a wagon moving between villages, moving much slower through time, and now time is mulchy and deep, getting peatier by the second. I can smell cow shit and hedgerow flowers. So I tell the driver that such a question—*How do you live with it?*—would be needing two responses. At least. He should choose. I can be the officious but repentant sin-eater for the English empire or I can be a Connaught orphan, weeping into his muddied hands. *How do I live with it? With unconscious consequence, I'm sure. And there's not a country on the earth where some kind of horror show like this hasn't happened. Cain-addled as we are.*

He pulls the horses over and he sings me a song. He says it's a song he sings at the golf club sometimes. He tends to drink Heineken in wineglasses with his wife now, but before lockdown he used to be up at the club once or twice a week. And you were not anything amongst his friends unless you could sing a song or tell a story. The wagon man's voice is clear and quite high, a wee bit of the chorister.

I quickly realise it's "On Raglan Road" he's about, the Patrick Kavanagh poem that was made a song by the Dubliners and others.[1]

> *O I loved too much and by such, by such,*
> *is happiness thrown away.*

> *I gave her gifts of the mind,*
> *I gave her the secret sign that's known*
> *To the artists who have known the true gods*
> *of sound and stone . . .*

He would be wrecking me, even this early in the day. I ask him which of my replies he'll accept, and he says: *Both. I trust the tension in them. That's mighty.* We get to the airport in the wagon that is a taxi again, and he jumps out and hugs me. He looks more like Christy Moore now, a giant of the island.

I'm glad that you're sorry. For what you did, and for leaving too. I forgive you for both of these things.

I can't say his words didn't have power to them. *It's good to be sorry, and for me to see that you're sorry.* And there, on the taxi rank of Dublin Terminal 2 at six-thirty in the morning, something deep has happened. The Master of the Wagon happily takes the English notes I give him, and he steams off into the flow of traffic, swearing and singing. The spirit has gone back to wherever he came from.

I've written that we recognise God in the eccentricity of our conscience. I'm interested in that thought. Not the usual, broad-stroke pangs—*forgetting to pay a debt, giving someone a slagging privately*—but subtler dimensions that maybe no one else notices. Those moments when you sprinkle a little bit of devilment into a conversation, choosing to abide in the murk, chuck some shade, impulsive but dark-seed sowing. I let myself off the hook for this most my life, I'm ashamed to say, but I have to keep shorter account now, being a God-Botherer and all.

Guilt can be complex, guilt can be simple. Sometimes, like the journey to Dublin Airport, it requires more than one response. I most definitely understand the need for confession in a way I didn't used to. If you also have half a wing curled, concealing something, spit it out. Don't keep the sickness in you. We damage others that way. Confession—in a prayer or speaking to someone you've wronged, or both—shifts us from guilt to remorse, and remorse brings repentance, *is* 90 per cent of repentance, really.

Some of Yeshua's prayers are so simple—the ones around exorcism especially—*Get out of him!* I always feel a twinge when he says that, that something is attempting to exit *me*, even as I read his words. And maybe something is. Excessive guilt, unattended and unrepented, is a grievous thing to carry. It will make us ill and limit the good we can do in the world.

One form of praying would be to go to a wood where no one is around. Dig a hole—with your paws—deep enough to rest your mush (face) in. Say the thing that cannot be said. Say it three different ways if you need to, but say it. Shout it or whisper it or weep it. Soil, trees, leaves, God delights in these things. It's the most natural thing imaginable to speak to him this way. Sometimes a small hole in the dirt is the only confessional we need. Our prayers will land this side of the river if we don't do the gritty, personal accounting. Guilt is always pointing to a course corrective and we have a God who tells us the door to mercy is still open. There's nothing he hasn't heard from humans' lips. Nothing.

To paraphrase Rumi: *How wonderful! Don't let a chance like this go by!*

I've been told many times that God recognises us by our grief, but I would suggest he also recognises us by our guilt—the fact we can even register such means he may be closer than we think. That it's pointing towards something redemptive. Responding to guilt is a creative act, requiring imagination and vulnerability. Our lives are thinner and much more concealed without it. They have less art in them, less reality, less God-contact. And as we finish, I circle back to the singing Irishman—it is through apology and restoration we ourselves are steadied and deepened, and finally enter into the heart-cracking rhythm of Kavanagh:

> *To the artists who have known*
> *The true gods of sound and stone*[2]

Without repentance, without *metanoia*, without getting *turned around*, I don't think such beings are quite revealed to us.

I'm going to finish this chapter with a wily old fairy tale, "The Six Swans." Guilt moves here and there within it, but the outcome is unexpected. Such stories are agile in how we can transmute paralysing emotions into something more useful. There's an alchemy at work here, something even the medieval hermits would wave their potions at—carefully.

There was once a king out hunting. As the day unfolded, pursuit of a deer utterly overwhelmed him. Farther and farther into the vast forest he rode, until his men had to abandon trying to keep pace. As they dropped away, he didn't notice. It was only when dusk caught up with him that he slowed his horse and realised he had become utterly lost. In fact it seemed the trees had swept the path behind him completely away. From every angle there were just tangled briars and gnarly oaks. It was not just alarming but humiliating; it was not good for a king to become so lost. He felt shame and some guilt over his incompetence. Did he even deserve his title?

Suddenly there was an old woman standing in front of him. Her head bobbed a little and it was hard to make out her expression in fast-darkening air.

When asked if she would show him a way home, she replied that she would only assist if he was to take her daughter for his bride. If he refused, he would never find the way out of such a tangling. She clearly had more than a little to do with the choreography of his situation. In a panic the king agreed, and was led to a hut that the witch and her daughter lived in. A fire was already lit, with the daughter standing by to meet him, the king having the strangest sensation she was already expecting his presence. Beautiful though she surely was, a chill note sounded in his heart. But, feeling the peril of the moment, he kept to his word and brought her back to his castle, the woods revealing a bright path back to hearth and home. The witch watched them disappear into the darkness, the trees then concealing the way back to her hut. No lit trail anymore. Contract signed.

The king and the daughter married, and all the kingdom celebrated, but still a low-down dread hung around him. He had things to protect. Years before, his previous wife, now dead, had borne them seven children: six boys and a girl. As a precaution he kept his children secret from the new queen. He squirrelled them off to a lonely tower in the woods, visiting whenever he could, but saying nothing to his new bride. It was a marriage of many concealments.

Again the forest rearranged and contorted its pathways, so the king brought with him a magical ball of twine that would show him back and forth from the tower when he threw it in front of him. And for a while, that was how life went.

But of course, the new queen was nothing if not observant. And noticing her husband's frequent trips into the forest, she determined to investigate. She found a servant susceptible to flattery, bribes, and a large serving of the king's brandy. She even got her chill hands on that most crucial aid: the ball of twine. She didn't like the sound of the children, not one bit. From hereditary witchcraft she fashioned silk shirts with little lumps of iron secreted within and laced them with spell-craft. She then waited till the king was off hunting, and she let the ball of twine lead her directly to the children.

Peering down from the tower's window, the children could only dimly make out the hooded figure walking towards them, and being their father was their only visitor, they presumed it was him. Only the daughter held back. But the boys, like excited puppies, ran down the echoing stone stairs and out into the dark grasses towards the shadowy being.

As they got within reach, she hurled shirts over each of them. As the iron and the silk landed on the boys, they turned into swans and flew away. In all the fluttering melee, the queen presumed her terrible work was done and turned to the castle. If she had looked back, she would have seen a girl in the shadows staring at a sky full of swans. It was a terrible night she spent alone in the tower. She was flooded with guilt that she hadn't been taken like her brothers.

In the morning her father visited, and his daughter told him everything. Distraught, he naturally wanted her to return with him, but she had no intention of being anywhere near the queen. Though she didn't realise who the hooded figure was, all instinct told the daughter not to return to the castle. The king reluctantly agreed for her to have one more night in the tower, thinking the brothers may even return in that time, for who knew the peculiar twists of forest magic?

She walked round and round in the tower until she couldn't bear it for a moment longer. She had to *do* something. So she struck out, looking for her brothers. Through the nettles and bushes, over the muddy streams and through ghostly copses, she looked all through the cold night and well into the next afternoon, when finally she came across the hut of woodsmen. She peered in and saw six beds. Cautiously she crawled under one of them to get a little rest. At dusk she was woken by a commotion, and when she peered out from under the bed she saw something wonderful: six swans landing, shaking themselves down and becoming her brothers again. They would blow at each other's feathers, and the swan skins would peel off, like a shirt.

Delightedly she crawled out from under the bed, and merrily the brothers greeted their beloved sister. However, there was a binding to the situation they had to reveal.

Dear sister. The problem is this. We can only regain our human shapes at dusk every night, for just fifteen minutes. We have just this precious moment as the sky turns from red to black, and then we are swans again. She grew agitated at this: *Is there really nothing that can be done, nothing at all?* The eldest brother looked grave. *The price is too high,* he said. *To break the spell, someone would have to make six shirts of aster flower—one for each us—and during that time remain utterly silent, putting all focus into the work. If they were to speak, all the intention would be lost, and the labour would be lost. Six long years it would take. As you can hear, the price is too high for anyone to pay.* After warning her not to spend the night at the hut—it belonged to robbers—he and his brothers became swans again, and sadly flew up and away, leaving her alone in the forest and the darkness.

But it was a different world now. Frightening and arduous, yes. Lonesome and uncertain, yes. But to hell with it. Now she had a quest.

She found a big tree and spent the night sheltering underneath. In the morning she started to gather aster flowers and began work. It was a delicate artistry she was apprenticing to, with many failures up ahead, many shirts simply coming apart in her hands. This happened again and again. Day after day she worked, and these long days became painstaking months. It was not difficult to remain silent as there was no one to talk to, and she was not in a mood for gaiety. After a time she felt safer working up on the branches of her big tree, and, if really absorbed, she got more moonlight up there to continue her work. Her fingers grew stronger daily, and also more subtle in their weavings.

But that kind of focus attracts people. In the daughter's case it attracted another king. One even more powerful than her father: king of the entire country. He was hunting in her part of the forest. His huntsmen called up to her in a friendly manner, promising no harm if she came down to join their picnic, but she was shocked at hearing voices after such a long time. Thinking them to be robbers, she threw down her gold necklace, then her girdle, garters, in fact everything she had on but her shift. This rather confused the huntsmen.

The king called up the tree in every language he knew—which was a considerable number—and most of all in a barely concealed love language of his own heart. She was like nothing he had ever come across before. Whilst not breaking her silence, she allowed herself to descend the tree and, with her work, come back to the castle with him.

For a time all was well. The king was quite accepting of both his beloved's silence and her work; they married and he was delighted when she grew pregnant. But his mother was less convinced—a woman found up a tree who never speaks? Who just makes shirts constructed from flowers every day? A witch, surely. When the daughter had their first child, the mother stole it away and smeared chicken blood on the sleeping woman's face.

Cannibal! Cannibal! Cannibal!

But the king would not chant along, horrified though he was, and protected his wife from his mother and the horrifying rumours. For her part, the daughter threw herself yet more fervently into her deep silence and her shirt-making.

Twice more she bore a child, twice more they were spirited away by the mother, chicken blood smeared on her lips, and utter defamation of her character called from rooftop to rooftop. A bereft and terrified king could defend his wife no more. She was condemned to be burnt at the stake.

But even in the dungeon she worked on the shirts, even as they brought her through the crowds to her burning, she was twisting and assembling the flowers, doing her very best to remain undistracted.

It happened that the execution was to take place on the last day of the six years she had been working. It happened that all six shirts were complete save one arm on the final shirt. As a servant bent to spark up the kindling, as she had the shirts laid on her arm, all heard a wild commotion.

Flying towards her from all directions were six swans, swooping over the heads of the astonished crowds, making the fiercest cries you could imagine. Each one dropped down in front of her, and as they passed she threw shirts on their backs. Soon she was flanked by her six ferocious brothers—one who would forever have the wing of a swan. And she spoke:

Now.
Now I have a voice. Now I have a story.
My mother-in-law
Took my children
Smeared my mouth
With chicken blood.

Her husband nearly passed out there and then. The queen was brought forward, and all saw the truth of the matter and the weight in the young queen's words. The children were found unharmed, and the mother received the punishment she had gleefully allotted for her daughter-in-law. Those who know say that from that day on, it was not unusual to hear the queen's voice singing up in the minstrels' gallery or by the hearth telling a story. It was a life of exultation she lived with her six brothers, her children, and her husband—it was a life in full disclosure.

GETTING LOST

Cultures, communities, mothers, sons, lovers get lost in the woods, and sometimes have to make monstrous bargains to get out alive. And the king knows it and feels the chill in his heart even as the beauty strolls towards him. Fairy tales often begin by circling around someone compromised and the nature of the decisions they make under such pressure. If not pressure, then simple distraction.

Kings are not meant to be "overwhelmed" by the hunt; they are the Lord of the Hunt. They are not meant to lose contact with their entourage and charge off. That is both reckless and dangerous for the wider culture of which they are the centre. Being king is not necessarily an erotic or creative proposition, because despite the king's stature, that role is defined by being of service to the land and the people. And that requires a cool head. Some storytellers describe this scene as the king having hunted too *hotly*.

Whilst generative in temperament, the mythic sovereign has also learnt to say the word *no*. Even to their own impulse system. They don't inflame easily. They can establish defences, hold the city through siege, patiently negotiating the most inflammatory of disputes. At least that's the old idea. That some of heaven's reasonableness shines through their character.

Of course the king has lost his wife; he's not balanced, and neither is the kingdom. Wouldn't you hurriedly pack the kids away? It's hardly their fault this is happening. But there's something so remote about the tower in the forest. How do they feed themselves? There's no trail of clues. Fairy tales often leave out much for us to conjure.

The king has a few magical smarts in his possession, most notably the ball of twine. The ball of twine orientates us to the vital: In the changing fortunes of the world it is a directive to stay connected to what *matters*. So it is a matter of terrible theft when someone else has dominion over it. If something else has your ball of twine, then you can't orientate to meaning. Addiction will steal the twine, crippling self-doubt, or stultifying depression. Professors can steal your twine, record executives, gurus. Excessive guilt can squirrel it away. William Stafford, a fine and subtle poet, said that the twine wasn't to be tugged on, but handled gently, and with curiosity. Otherwise it splits apart in our anxious fist.

THE SWANS

Not lions, not bears, not hawks; swans. What does a boy turned into a swan look like? Could it be a useful maturation? Over the last sixty years of commentary on the tale there has often been a comparison between the swan boys and the lofty notion of the *puer aeternus*. The bright one, prone to inspirational brilliance but averse to the hard labour of building much. The bright one is a leap, but not a bridge. They are more comfortable in the air or sailing on glittering stretches of water than on boring earth. Of course, there are any number of *puellas* too. To their credit, puers are wonderful at kick-starting inspiration when the conversation is stodgy, but their eyes grow cloudy when the nuts and bolts of the proposed endeavour are discussed. I know I was one of these characters, though life has diligently dished out prolonged hidings as a successful cure.

The puer never stops talking, so what's required for us to soulfully deepen? To stop talking. We are six swans out in the world a great deal of the time, posting our best self on social media, nodding meaningfully to the next spiritual fad, sucking chamomile through a hemp straw, but there is another part of ourselves alone in the quiet of an ancient wood, silently working with our hands on a great task. The story tells us that is the part of us that is going to save us. Many years on the hill guiding wilderness vigils has acquired me contact with many such shirt-making sisters.

Marie-Louise von Franz has spent time thinking about this story.[3] She assembled some wonderful details about swans; that the word swan has the same root as the Latin *sonare*, meaning "sound" or "sounding." So to become a swan is to be connected to a kind of sounding. A kind of voice. She also discovered that through German folk tradition the bird was meant to know the future, had a prophetic agency. But mythically it has more than one aspect. To von Franz, the swan could be a winged flight away from all the good, earthy qualities of our humanity, but in a more positive aspect a great illumination of consciousness and eroticism.

She also noted that swans grow gradually weaker as they age and sometimes starve to death out there on the ice. Their famed "swan song" can have a rather brittle quality to it. A life where the puer takes dominion can also lead to bitterness at the end. The world will never quite live up to our flighty, golden expectations, and we never really dove deep enough to taste its worldly insights. Life demands the puer give up its essential naivety. This is not a new idea, but the repetition required to get the message is quite astounding.

Swans, witches, children in towers. They are in a *communicato*, they are *designed* to bump into each other. Myth is a contact sport. All of them left entirely alone risk frozen remoteness, but in dynamic proximity to one another become vital and provocative. That proximity is the lairy mosh pit of our own character, the swirling holy world around us, and the infinite threads between.

INITIATORY SILENCE

For fifteen minutes a day we can think straight. For fifteen minutes we can extract ourselves from enchantment and communicate something more than a trance state. I once knew a poet who claimed all his poems were just those fifteen minutes sewn together. Of course the directive for the swan boys' sister is grievous. To remain silent as she sews shirts of aster flower for each of them, an incredibly skilled undertaking without the implied solitude being stacked on top. It seems hopeless, designed to come apart in our hands over and over again.

If you ever work with young people, you may want to try telling them that whatever the task is they are doing, it's likely hopeless. That it's never been achieved. What else is worth doing? She has a craft to learn, and this will not be a community endeavour. She will not be sitting with her girlfriends in the castle smiling and laughing. This is knowledge of the deep interior that's being called for at this moment. It has a related quality to when a man is instructed not to wipe the tears from his eyes, or to cut the hair from his head. This particular gradient of silence is not a mandate for patriarchy or any such thing, but it invokes a limit to assist sufficient deepening. As we've seen, in myth, something usually has to be taken away for something else to grow.

Can you remember what it feels like to have something come apart in your hands, again and again? The shame in that? The flush of the cheek and the resolve to continue even as you burn with embarrassment. There is no distance left to run, you simply have to stay with it. Within fairy tales, silence can have a variety of qualities and is substantial in its power and influence. When words *are* formed, they come from the pathos of the weight of the space around them. It's not just rat-a-tat-tat. Initiatory silence has the quality of the brood whilst the eggs incubate; it has less spillage, it's refined, there's more acuity to its aim.

It's a dimension that religious orders and mystical folk the world over understand. I know a young African girl who deliberately goes into silence once a week for a full day, to steady herself. Confirm her own fundament. It's to do with a certain deliberateness, a kind of yoga of the soul. It's not secrecy but privacy. We get thinned out without it, and much easier to fool.

Silence in initiatory circumstance is rarely passive: It is a gathering in. Silence in this arrangement is fidelity to the deep interior, an end to chatter and the push-pull of the market square. It is a kind of virginity. It is the end of influence. Such a silence gathers up gleams of light from the Otherworld in the folds of its skirt.

It's a quality I see in my mother, and it's possible I step in and out of it myself on a good day. A quality of incubation before potent birthing of language. There is a hysteria to constant verbal communication that bleeds our words of heft. The trill of banter that eventually fills our mouth with feathers not corn.

TO CARRY A SWAN'S WING

The one wing is the loose thread on the Persian rug, the grit in the oyster, the reminder that we don't quite live in Paradise. Some claim the one-winged amongst us are those that best remember their lives as swans. Having one wing is going to deny us complete practicality, and is a little ungainly. We didn't quite skip through the initiation like the others. But it could be argued that a certain heavenly door is kept open in such an individual, whose art delights and nourishes others. The Pakistani singer Nusrat Fateh Ali Khan was such a character.

At the end of this story I find myself asking what disasters sank me into guilty silence, and what provoked me into initiatory silence? As we have seen, there's all the difference in the world.

A tale that began with guilt has, after an enormous amount of labour, ended in a marriage of full disclosure. I would wish that for all of us. Initiatory silence is by no means the same as the guilty silence held by the bee monk at the beginning of the chapter. That kind rots you from the inside. In "The Six Swans," however, the silence is productive; something is literally being woven from it. It's a task that not only frees her brothers but gifts her a full and powerful voice, an earned voice. Her own story has been gathered in, her guilt transmuted to purpose, and the fullness of her commitment has indeed brought her—through the most hazardous of challenges—home.

9

ON ENVY

As a young lad I had a whole heap of envy, every which way I looked. Self-reliant I was not. I thought everyone was better off than me. Not a good look. More handsome, brighter, cash to flash. Terrible at sports, a natural loner, I glowered a bloodshot eye at the world and sniffed and sulked and hobbled back to my library, thinking complicated thoughts. I was sure if I ever met Bob Dylan he would *definitely* get me, but until then I had to tough it out. I kept my mind full of fable and flash and tried to ignore my dismal surrounds. I had winklepicker boots and big hair, and that was a start.

Envy these days tends to take me by surprise. Mercifully, it's not an address I spend an awful lot of time at. Significant stretches can pass and it simply doesn't come up. There's a lot in my life to be grateful for, a fairly coherent narrative to cleave to. That in itself creates regular encounters with meaning, which then in turn regulates what the Sufis call the *Nafs*, or "the greedy soul." Life is absorbing, and in that absorption I break free of the illusion of scarcity. When I feel scarcity it's usually coming from a wound or some maleficent trance I've fallen under. Envy takes us far from home.

Envy's a horrible motel to stay at. The pizza is cold, the air sour, there's a party going on down the hall and you most definitely do not have an invitation. No one wanders down your end of the corridor. It's a master class in smallness, and distinctly uncreative. When it does come upon me, I feel stiffed by the world, stiffed by God, and under the restrictions of some preordained cosmological limit. And this will always be instigated by staring too long into a neighbour's field. So-and-so garners more respect in the world, so-and-so seems award-adorned, so-and-so can't move for the sheer, rather irritating, level of opportunity in their life.

I become a Grendel, listening at the door of the feasting hall and knowing the cheers and toasts are not for me. The mermaids will not be singing for me. The world becomes sepia-tinged, and I head off into hurt, mostly self-inflicted isolation. I brood, and at my worst, I slag whoever happens to be in my sights that day. Whoever the garlanded one is allotted to be this time.

This state is pure devilment. It is to be nipped in the bud and to be indulged as briefly as possible. When I'm in this place I have no largesse in me, no charity, and I feel very far from everybody.

Marie-Louise von Franz made a brilliant observation about evil.[1] She said in the old stories there were both hot and cold varieties. Hot evil is the realm of the Giant: externally destructive, swinging a club, demolishing villages, roaring, wrathful. It's a loud kind of wickedness, easy to sketch; you can see it smouldering down the path towards you. Cold evil is subtler; cold evil is not the realm of the Giant but the Witch. The Witch traffics in isolation, getting you alone in the forest, thinning out any sense of relatedness to the wider world. It's a condition of ice and remove. Envy takes me to a place of tremendous cold, not heat. And on that island of remove, we can become prey to the illusionary:

In my solitude, I have seen many things that were not true.

ANTONIO MACHADO[2]

We can read Machado's line several ways, but I'd work with it like this: Rather than something profound sifting to consciousness, and falsehood falling away, solitude here is the icky realm of indulging the hurt and fantastical. We don't know the inner story of whoever today's garlanded one happens to be. We don't know their troubled backstory, their inhibitions and self-loathing, we haven't wandered a mile in their boots. They become the latest revolving-door symbol of our sense of lack. We resent feeling passed over or scuffed by the world—of course we do—but we simply can't set up shop there. We are polluting our customers.

Disorder, as we know, is one of the great Luciferic blueprints. I'm not talking about a scruffy workstation (that's how I roll), but a persistent, nasty, divisive attention to chaos and breaking down connections. Us and them. Those bad Others. We must remember the Teacher with his hand drawing in the dust at such a moment. The old folklore insists that as we pick up the rock, he is drawing a list of our sins in the sand. Maybe we breathe, put the stone down, come back to our senses.

It's a big ask, Christianity; it's huge and difficult and mythological. A lot of what we call theosis is aided by the genius Irish phrase "Cop onto yourself." That's a divine mandate: You are baking loaves with something bad in them, no matter how sweet the smell.

In fairy tales envy is a place often inhabited by characters called the false brothers or sisters. There will be two siblings who are vain, self-absorbed, and easily wounded. There will be one who is more charitable, a humble character. I think this hints that at least two-thirds of our time we could be in the orbit of falsehood and malice, and we are to do the difficult religious work of attending to the lesser-seen qualities of the third brother or sister. And that one is largely less respected in the world initially. Charisma is probably not their thing, but quieter and maybe wholesome attributes.

A way out of Witch-energy is to talk to someone who you love and trust. Risk speaking of the struggle. It reduces the boil on the sizzling kettle, or unfreezes the ice. Greater things are calling us—further up and further in—and to spend another minute in the dung heap of this malaise is unfitting. It may be a prayer, it may be over a coffee or a pint, but speak of the smallness and watch it contract, lose charge.

My late friend Tony Hoagland and I provided this for each other. And we weren't hard on our hang-ups either. We asked for forgiveness and often ended up laughing at something that had us breathlessly constricted five minutes before. I remember his lines: *My need to control even the kindness of the world, rejecting gifts for which I am not prepared.* So much of what we envy, when it finally arrives, is not at all like what we expected. Negotiating guilt, diminishing envy, raising a kid—these have been royal roads to growth, each one a rite of passage if I just squint hard enough.

A story that teaches on envy is the marvellous Saami story "Akanida Daughter of the Sun."

———————————⁃●⁃———————————

And so it was that Akanida, daughter of the Sun, moved through the sky distributing warmth to the earth. She gave freely to all: to the trout of the silvered stream, the antlered herds of the taiga, even the peregrine in her spring flight felt Akanida's affection on her feathers. With her father's help, it was a family affair to keep the earth blessed by heat. It was Akanida who helped things thaw, bud, and drowsily blossom, and she felt the sheer gratitude of the earth emanate back to her in a thousand secretive ways.

It was humans she just couldn't figure.

They seemed fickle. Sometimes they laughed and danced and seemed grateful for her gifts; other times they retreated to their skin tents and brooded, sullen with each other. There were so many weather patterns within them, it made her curious. You couldn't quite pin them down. She wondered about their capacity for cruelty, and the strange things they found amusing, wondered about what made them grieve and what laws they stood by. She noticed that not everyone hunted or worked, but strangely the ones that did seemed to suffer the most. The chubby ones in sable skins were rarely seen driving the reindeer to lusher pastures; it was scruffy, skinny folks who did that, heads lolling with starvation. The furnace of her heart moved towards them most of all. The raggedy ones. It was them she wished to help. To bring happiness to the endless grind of their labours.

At the end of the day when he sank beneath the sea, she went to see her father the Sun. As usual he was exhausted and a little tetchy after his graft. Sparks flew from him as he tried to settle. Taking courage, she spoke up:

Father, I want to go down and live amongst the people, down on earth.

If it is possible to groan and snarl at the same time, the Sun did so. *Is the sky not vast enough for you to travel through? Why do you need to be down amongst the befuddlements of humans? They are changeable at the best of times. Better stay up here with the wind, I know you love to sing with the wind. The wind is a good friend to you.*

Hmm.

Akanida went into a kind of silence that all fathers recognise as particular to their daughters. Each daughter has a different kind of silence. Far more effective than just endless pleading. Once she had demonstrated this effectively, she calmly asked again. Maybe his defences were low after his labour, maybe he just loved her so, but this second time round he surprisingly agreed. *All right, all right. You can go. Rest up now, get some sleep, and travel down in the morning.* Akanida was beside herself with excitement.

When she woke, everything was utterly different. Her father was gone, her friend the wind was way high overhead, as were her companions the clouds.

She was lying on a reindeer hide in a tent. Her nostrils filled with the deliciousness of woodsmoke and a bubbling venison stew. Before her stood an astonished old man and woman, utterly agape. Childless they were, and now there was a young girl before them, face as round as a cloudberry, eyes as blue as the snow you pad over in the moonlight. She looked straight at them.

Let me live with you and be your daughter, said Akanida simply.

The old woman wrinkled her face and looked at the young girl with her spirit-eye, her deep knowing, and had an insight into exactly who it may be in front of them. She smiled broadly:

Of course, come and live with us just as you like. And with that, she did.

Quickly her curiosity took her from the tent and she started to explore. The tent was situated under a bent old pine tree, on a small island in the middle of Lake Svyato. Absolutely nobody was there but the kind old man and woman. Not a soul.

Akanida realised what her father was up to. The Sun was not without wit. Like any parent, he wished his daughter to be safe, and so had both honoured her request but had also sequestered her away from any possible trouble. She glanced up at the Sun overhead and sighed, waggling a finger. When she pleaded with the old folks to be let off the island, they told her that she was not even old enough to wear the headdress of a maiden, and that she must stay. But they also advised her to be patient, and that such a moment of departure would come soon enough. She listened to their counsel. Like a stone being slowly polished, or a staff being whittled into a new shape, she worked on patience. She applied herself.

She became a helper to the old woman and her tasks, and she would help the old man fix his nets at night. She became skilled at unpicking tangles. Time passed in this way. But things change in their time too.

You should know that when you become a maiden you are to wear a special dress, and with delight the old woman started to create such a thing for the girl. Akanida loved to see this dress developing, and happily contributed little stones to attach as bright colours, and dried fruit to function as gems. It soon became utterly lovely, the most ornate and wonderful of dresses, highly unusual. The old woman and the young girl would stay up late working on it whilst the old man watched, smiling at them through the smoke.

One day, at the appointed time, the old man carefully crafted Akanida a crown of juniper twigs, and the old woman dressed her in her maiden's robe. She had come of age.

She was so delighted she ran down to the water's edge to catch her reflection. So jubilant was she with what she saw, she started to dance, and for the first time she sang. Her voice carried a winged cadence: There were flutters and trills and inventive bends that took the breath clean away from the old couple. When she sang, nightingales nested in the sound, leaves fell delicately from the birch, the reindeer stamped her proud hoof on crisp snow. All of creation was present when she sang. It was quite wonderful.

The old couple looked at each other astonished, and a truth announced itself to them. The man spoke: *We can't have her all to ourselves anymore. It's time she met the people and sang her song, to open their ears and their eyes.* And the old woman shuffled forward, and in the words of her people gave Akanida her blessing into womanhood. May all our daughters be so lucky.

That night, a strong wind picked up and the tent flapped wildly and the gnarly old pine groaned with duress; it bent its bough until the whole island moved northward through the rippling lake to the bank of the land. It was at the mouth of a great river, called the River of Our Fathers.

In the morning, Akanida did not need a canoe; she stepped directly onto the mainland. Happily and a little proudly, the old man took her to meet the people. With her, Akanida carried three small suede bags, sewn herself and decorated with coloured stones and dried fruit.

They arrived at the tents of some Saami folk. Raising the flap of a skin tent, they peered in through the rising smoke and saw a happy scene. There was a group of people tucking into whale meat, the fat glistening on their chins: The sea had been especially kind to them, gifting them many days, even months, of meat. The waves had pushed a mountain of ice to the mouth of the river, and within it they had found a frozen whale. They hacked it free, and it was its meat they were enjoying as the travellers arrived.

When they saw Akanida, they all clambered to their feet and crowded round her. The women caressed her cheeks, the men hugged her to their chest, and the beaming kids all attempted to clamber up on her lap, all at once. In some fashion, everyone made contact with her: touched a braid or the hem of her skirt, smiled a shy smile or held her close. It was the most beautiful of welcomes, but a little boisterous maybe.

In the melee, Akanida uttered a magical word, a word never revealed to human ears before, and suddenly no one could touch her; their hands passed right through her. She was completely still, didn't move, but no one could gain purchase on her form. This alarmed the people, but she calmed them and called them all out of the tent, and told them to walk hand in hand to the riverbank, where she then started to dance and sing.

So astonishing was the incantation that all started to sing her song and take up the dance as best they could. After a long time they collapsed, utterly fatigued from the exertion. Whilst nobody was looking, Akanida slipped a handful of berries and stones from her suede bags and laid them on the soil. She called the young ones from the rest, and placed her hand over her treasury. *What do I have under my hands?* she asked. *Nothing,* they replied. She smiled and lifted her palms.

> *There was a*
> *Patterning of circles*
> *Wheels within wheels*
> *Suns and Moons*
> *The feet of Magpie*
> *The feet of Goose*
> *All a-glitter in benevolent sunlight*

In the astonishment, she spread out all the berries and stones and encouraged the people to try their own pattern-making. Well, they tried, and with reasonable results, but nothing like the agility of

Akanida. She gathered them under her slim hands again: Her next step was to ration out the contents of her suede bags to the women, to decorate their clothes and boots with ornate patterns. They just adored their new work and would bring it for her to see. She would make suggestions, to just tune up its shape a little. *Next time you will do no worse*, she would say, and nuzzle their cheeks. The women would admire themselves in the reflection of the lake, and their menfolk were delighted too—such beauty! Soon the young men were assisting them in the maintenance of such incredible clothes. And Akanida's work did not stop there. She started to travel from tent to tent and then camp to camp. She would cut a hollow stem and fashion a flute, making an exquisite sound, or would dance or sing, and was always opening her suede bags and encouraging the people to start making patterns from the glittering bounty. In this way she brought joy and contentment to the Saami.

It was her songs they sang when they mended their nets, got their kids to rest, celebrated or feasted: tales of the ice mountain and the whale, songs of the sun, moon, and stars, incantations of generous good fortune when hunting. At night they gathered by the sparkling fire and commenced with her dances, shuffling and swirling. They relished what she had brought just like they relished the warmth of the sun.

Well, almost all did.

Into every story a little rain must fall.

The elders hung back a little. Were not convinced. Lips pursed. They folded their ears to her songs like the flaps of a tent against a blizzard, bundled up their hearts as a babe against the frost, heated up their minds like a hunter makes fire against her rituals. They would not let her in.

But she had something they wanted, so they kept their grumbles to themselves, held out their hands and cried:

Bring us more gems.

So she did. And they said again, *Bring us more gems.* It never stopped; it was relentless, ugly, their requests simply never abated. Gradually she realised what was happening. It was not for love or ritual abundance they requested gems, not for noble deeds or just to decorate clothes, but for trade: boots, rugs, weapons, and the hides of squirrel and reindeer.

They got fat on her charity, just like the chubby ones she'd spied from the sky. Welcome to the full range of the human situation.

So she stopped handing out the berries and stones, and immediately the old ones gathered up their malice in great bundles and threw it in her direction. Then they turned and addressed the people themselves:

Why do you sing these songs? And preen by the lake all day when you should be hunting? What are all these patterns? We never needed them before. She has turned us from our own traditions, our own ways. We must rid ourselves of Akanida.

But it would serve greedy people well to remember exactly who Akanida's father was. With his radiant protection she was unkillable. But the old ones weren't done speculating on how to cause her damage.

They dragged a reindeer carcass down to a lonely place, a swamp, where lurked a powerful witch, Oadz. Her songs and customs they understood well from way back. Very different songs. There were many ancient arrangements threaded between her and the elders. But no one came to the swamp anymore to listen to her songs, not since the arrival of Akanida. Oadz was out of favour, and you can be sure to bet a thousand elk skins she didn't like it. With the libation offered, Oadz slid up woefully, terrifyingly, and gnashingly out of the black mud and hissily agreed to help. She crooned:

Take a stone the colour of green moss. Seal up the smoke flap on Akanida's tent so the Sun cannot see her, and hurl the stone at her. It'll kill her.

Eagerly the elders collected a moss-green stone and went to the woman's tent. As was so often the case, they found Akanida surrounded by children, showing them how to create buttons out of shells. In their eagerness for her utter destruction, they forgot an essential ingredient: They neglected to seal the smoke hole. The blow from the stone grievously winded Akanida as it thwupped her chest, but it didn't kill her.

In front of the startled children she started to fade, but as she faded she sang a powerful song, of such impact the song itself grew wings and beat out a pattern on the walrus skins in front of her. The whole tent became a huge pulsing drum as she sang, and the souls of the people felt just like the rising smoke, like they were approaching heaven; such were the ecstasies of her parting song. As the song completed itself, Akanida entered the spiralling smoke and left the tent, travelling up towards the sky and the glad presence of her father.

You should know that to this day she has not returned to earth. But the work she came to do blossomed amongst the Saami. The people did not return to the swamp-ways and the claustrophobic chants of wicked old Oadz, and the bog became a place forgotten. She's still there though, biding her time.

No. The people continued to sing Akanida's songs, enact her dances, create beauty in their clothes and very character, work deeper into her patterns, even make their own every once in a while. Mothers pass her sunny wisdoms to their daughters, fathers to sons, and there are now stories everywhere: under every rock, tucked away in any bough of larch, and sweetly lurking in a child's mouth—stories to temper and soften the heart, to surround the people even in the fiercest of winters, the deepest kind of binding against the cold. When his day's work is done, the Sun stands with his daughter Akanida, and they blaze happily with light, and gaze down on the good that she has made.

THE ENVY OF THE GODS

Our inconstancy is fascinating to the gods. The brief flare-up of our years, our pettiness and fidelities all hold their attention. The fleetingness of life is mesmeric, erotic in a way. There's something rather unsexy about eternity. They say their storytellers weave their epics through the drama of our own narratives. It's said they are bored witless with their apportioned lot. They even envy us.

In this story, Akanida, a divinity who distributes her father's warmth, is particularly captivated. In her fascination she finds another way to dish out sustenance, by the rituals and dances she brings to the people. She makes culture.

It takes a while to develop human patience, but she does so, applying herself to the tasks of the hut, even whilst her crafty father has found a way to both honour her wishes and keep her safe for a while. Dads do this kind of thing. A tent with an old couple on a solitary island is hardly Times Square. But this is a world that still has tacit awareness of the divine. She is discreetly recognised by the old woman and allowed to stay under their roof.

A question: What has arrived in our lives that we recognise as significant, even holy, and how do we feed it and raise it? Did it wither or flourish?

The story tells us that what arrives needs space and quiet around it. And that over time it needs to be grounded in tasks particular to the lived, human experience. If it elected to show up, then it may need a little tuition in the ways of this world. This happens again and again in these stories. So how does a deity come of age? How can we help a spiritual force mature? Is that even possible? It needs craft, repetition, instruction.

The beginning of the story provokes many questions. There is something delightful about the scene of the old woman and Akanida quietly working on the dress as the old man smiles across at them. In Russian stories it is said that a woman needs ten thousand feminine secrets sewn into her wedding dress before she marries. The wiles of the old lady are flooding into it at the same time as the generative overview of the heavens.

So the story dictates its tempo. With the creation of the dress, and the blessing of the old woman, change arrives. Rooted in the feminine, she is brought-by-storm to the masculine, the River of our Fathers. I wonder what such a storm would look like to our daughters. What storm leads them from adolescence to young womanhood? There is something extraordinary about a deity undergoing a human rite of passage. Maybe even the gods seek to be witnessed by us, sometimes.

The Saami are delighted to see her, almost too excited, so she reveals that she is in the world but not quite of it: They can't quite lay their excited hands on her. She's not a plaything. She has much to give, but not in a melee. The rough-and-tumble of our world needs a little divine organisation, needs to comprehend a boundary or two. There is something childish in their response to her, something that needs education.

What she brings is patterns. Organised, delightful, formal patterns. She brings form. She distributes a kind of refreshment-through-ceremony to the wider tribe, but in this case, the betrayal of such kindness will come a little later.

From the French caves to a Moroccan mosque to a Hackney synagogue to an Orkney kirk, humans delight in ornamentation as divine celebration, as diverse as the cultures that birthed them. In such places the move from making beauty to being beauty can occur. The making itself makes us beautiful. The strong fingers that invoke the images in an Aboriginal sand painting become part of the dream divining of the creation itself.

But it can't stay this way, can it? Even when the holy fire moves from tent to tent, showing us how to live. Trouble always lopes in, spitting and sniffing the air, cocking its hind leg. We have to leave Eden and make the best of it out here with the plastic sofas, cheap promises, and barbed wire. Where else is there to lay our prayer mat?

SEALING THE SMOKE HOLE

Innocence can never be the whole story. Envy shows up in the so-called elders. The ones not crone-tasty, but hag-sour. The ones who hang out in the damp of the swamp reviving stagnant energies. Sealing the smoke hole is quite a terrifying image. To create invisibility from divine eyes so killing can occur. To break the connection. It is possible for life's brutality to close the smoke hole in our soul to the heavenly world. And that's not just a place of the seemingly far away, it's a place of pine cones and bullish storms and antler-clashed stags among humming dark grasses. It's vivid and magical and filled with communication.

And for countless thousands of years we have gazed out at the earth or up into the heavens and witnessed presences looking back at us. That maybe even wished us well every now and again. We lose the old arrangement when we seal the smoke hole. Grief becomes despair, wit becomes sarcasm, the world can be measured. Climate change is a result of culturally sealing the smoke hole. Not just to some far-distant heaven but the heaven that roams in and around and through us. Seal up the smoke hole and on the deepest, most unconscious level, nothing matters. Seal up that hole and we become mad. Seal up that hole and the most ruthless of acts can be reasoned into actuality. We become possessed by ourselves, and only ourselves.

The God I follow has things to say about envy, and self-serving motivations. He offers a road that doesn't indulge peering at our neighbours' fields and fuming with our supposed lack. For you and I trying to get home, to become real human beings, to gather our thrown-away stories, this is a radical step in the right direction. You can be a pious monk in fifth-century Egypt or a burlesque dancer in modern New York, but we all turn green sometime. Someone is our Akanida, someone evokes our smaller nature. There be monsters. Pat the gargoyle on the shoulder and tell it a story, I promise it will help. There are all sorts of accumulated hurt in us, all kinds of scuffs. A story helps settle the interior-den and brings these turbulent and evasive forces to the table. In my decades as a storyteller I have become much more honest. Stories are the most delightful vehicles for the brightening of consciousness. True, archaic technology.

10

ON DREAM

One night I dreamt it started to snow.

For a while it was charming, then it wouldn't stop. The sky, when briefly it was light, was a strange yellow colour, with large flakes chucking down. Then the darkness and the night would come again. I found myself inside the door of my parents' house, with a massive line of folk needing to take shelter. For a while it was chaos, with a dangerous amount of snow being stomped in or billowing through the door, being constantly opened to let in more of the vulnerable. The snow would melt into great pools of water and there was a danger of flooding. The free-form chaos needed shape, and once there was reminding of the ancient etiquette of the home, everybody calmed and there was suddenly space. The home could accommodate all, but there was an archaic mode of entry that had to be surrendered to, otherwise the dwelling could no longer offer shelter.

There were terms.

Some turned away, back out into the swirling dark.

It woke me at 5 a.m., this dream, and I sat in the dark with a flask of tea, writing it up. I don't pin dreams on the rack of endless interpretation, but I do give them space and attention. Even in the dream I knew it was a Green Chapel door the folks were walking through. The Green Chapel is a place where the valiant knight Gawain ends up when he has to honour the rules of a game he committed to play. He has to lose his head to find his life.

For me to approach the mythology of Christianity would have felt, for many years like losing my head. A faintly ridiculous thing to do. That, in the language of this very book, you had to surrender your life to find your life. To get home, to become a truly storied human, you walk through the narrow gate. Well, you can be sure, for long and rather chaotic decades, I felt no urgency to do that.

But then the snow came.

In this hazy-just-woken space I could hear the village bell strike six, which meant I must have drifted in and out for another hour. I'm remembering a book from my childhood (along with Alan Garner, the most significant of my early years)—Susan Cooper's *The Dark Is Rising*—in that there is a great peril when it starts to snow and won't stop. The snow—something I mostly love—becomes an agent of forces that do not wish us well. Profound mythological energies are invoked to protect what needs protecting.

Only the Ancient Good will do.

Quite what the Ancient Good is has to be furtively groped towards by each of us. I can certainly hint, but it's bad storytelling to knock you over the head with it. In this chapter I want to invite you to take your dreams seriously. That tempering can come in the moonlight as well as sunlit hours. Dreams are shifting inner-mythologies, prompting and provoking under the cloak of sleep. When we give them space and attention, unusual things can happen, as our next story reveals. I call it "John of the Dreams," though some will know it as "The Pedlar of Swaffham."

— ◆ —

In the village of Swaffham a man once had a dream. And in the dream a figure appeared in a red cloak and spoke a simple message:

Get yourself to London Bridge, fast as you can. Something good will happen.

The man, whose name was John, woke his wife Kath up and told her the dream. Kath was used to his dreams, and rather weary of them.

What good is a dream? A vision for your life would be better, but dreams aren't worth a thing.

Yes, I suppose a vision is better than a dream, said John sadly, and he went back to sleep.

Then he had the exact same dream again.

The next day he badgered everyone with it: the blacksmith, the weaver, the midwife, the baker, till all were sick of it. He worked his way across the village telling everyone till by dusk he arrived at the church. Terrible state it was: slates missing, walls crumbling, tower filled with crows and awfully wobbly. No bell. Mother Kirk was sick.

Weaving through gravestones came the priest, Master Fuller. In the half-light he listened to the pedlar's dream with watery blue eyes almost closed. He groaned in irritation:

We all bloody dream. They signify nothing. Figure a vision to rebuild the church! Now that would be something.

Tired Master Fuller gestured to the collapsed roof of the north aisle, the mossy walls. The priest then walked off into the gloom muttering loudly:

Dreams! As if dreaming ever did anything.

That night, over ale and by the fire with Kath, John started up on his dream again. Kath rose, and with that fierce old glint in her eye, said:

I'll never hear the end of this. Go on! Go. Go with God but go.

Next day the pedlar said goodbye to Kath and his children and set out with his hound, a jug of beer, and a bag of bread and cheese. He had five gold coins tucked away and a big walloping stick for anyone who came at him. For much of the first day he was surrounded by what he already knew: sheep in distant fields, smallholdings, woods, and the occasional fox. Walking like this was rather fun; he sipped his beer and sung out a song now and then.

But over time the landscape changed, grew less familiar.

Soon it was all heathland, with no happy curl of smoke from a cottage, no cheery wave from a farmer. This was land beyond his knowledge, and he grew quieter, more cautious. In time the beloved little tracks he'd known all his life ended, and he found himself on a bigger path that men called the Gold Road. Soon it was raining, soon it was dark, and he found himself kipping in a ditch, miserable and afraid. In the morning he was aching, sodden and filled with hunger.

It won't surprise you to know the next four days were more of the same. But, despite the discomfort, those days certainly weren't boring. His hound hobbled along loyally beside him as they travelled through ghoulish woods and endless miles of nothing much. They fell in with a pilgrim on his way to Jerusalem, met boozy youths on their way to the fair, even a beautiful young woman who attempted to sell him a ticket to heaven. At night, under whatever oak tree, inn, or monastery he was sheltering in, he wondered at all whom he'd met. His mind was wider and deeper than even a few days before. So much life to take in.

Finally he came to London. He smelt it before he saw it. Then he heard it. The smell was of unwashed bodies and sewage, the sound was of shouts, music, punch-ups, and laughter. Houses were built above houses, and the whole place swayed and shimmered in front of him. Folks of all shapes, sizes, colours, and dispositions. And most trying to flog him something. It was both terrifying and wonderful all at the same time.

The pedlar finally got to London Bridge, over the grey and swishing Thames. Suddenly he had no idea what to do. The dream wasn't terribly precise at this moment. Now a *vision*, that would have told him what to do. That would have been a map. He started to feel outrageously stupid. No one paid him a blind bit of notice. He'd hold a gaze just in case someone would nod and was "in-on-the-dream," but the days passed and nothing happened.

John would sit in the dust and watch the boats go by. He spent his coin on a night's lodgings and making a black bear dance, and soon it was all gone. He'd seen a group of cloaked pilgrims pass on their way to the Holy Land of Walsingham and he had a great surge of homesickness, Walsingham being a place he knew well. His sense of foolishness grew daily, and the dream seemed to get fainter. Could he even completely trust he hadn't made it up?

One day a shopkeeper walked over to him:

I've seen you sitting here for days. What on earth are you up to? You don't beg or steal. What are you doing?

Well, a dream told me I should come. That something good would happen.

Dreams! You idiot. You shouldn't hang your heart on dreams. I myself had a dream just last night. I dreamt of a village called Swaffham, and in it a garden that belonged to a pedlar, and in that garden a hawthorn tree. And in the dream, buried by the tree was a pot filled with gold. That wouldn't make sense to anyone, would it?

The pedlar's head began to swim. He thanked the baffled shop-keeper and began to run in the direction of Swaffham, his happy hound at his ankles.

John headed in the opposite direction of the Gold Road, and his eyes filled with tears when he finally saw the little tracks and fields of sheep and tiny copses he'd loved his whole life. He burst into his cottage wild-eyed and mud-splattered to his beloved Kath and told her the whole story. She thrust his old spade in his hand, and they ran out to the hawthorn tree and he started to dig. At first there was nothing:

How odd to leave with one dream and return with another's, muttered Kath.

Soon there was the satisfying clunk of metal on metal, and he indeed dragged up a pot filled with gold from the dark soil. Beside themselves, they carried the pot inside and sat there breathlessly counting the money. In the half-light they noticed there was some-thing written in Latin around the lid. They would need someone who could decipher it. That night they slept with the gold stacked up in the bedroom, glowing at the foot of their bed. Every now and then one of them would wake and dreamily marvel at the fortune.

The next day they called over Master Fuller the priest. He warily surveyed the pedlar and noted he hadn't seen him in church that Sunday.

Well, I was . . . er . . . out and about, Father, said John, playing for time. *I was wondering if, with your book smarts, you could tell us what is written on this pot?*

The priest put on his spectacles, peered at the inscription, and read the Latin: *Under me is someone richer!*

Kath and John stared at each other. With Kath keeping the priest occupied with tea and cake, the pedlar and his kids nipped out to the hawthorn tree and started to dig. This time it was his kids, Maggie and Hugh, who got to share the labour. They toiled and toiled, great clods of mud flying over them, till there was the satisfying clunk of metal on metal. There was another pot, at least twice as large as the last one. John spoke:

This is a dream. But a dream I can stand up and walk around in. A dream that has changed the shape of our lives forever.

And suddenly he knew what he had to do with the money from the second pot.

He walked back into the house where the priest and Kath were chatting. He noticed how threadbare the priest's robes were, and how thin he'd got.

Father, how much gold would we need to fix old Swaffham Church?

The father smiled sadly:

More than any of us have or can lay our hands on. I love the old place, but it seems its time is up. The bell no longer rings, no pilgrims attend.

Would you come into the garden, please? I have something to show you.

And with that, the priest, the pedlar, Kath, Maggie, and Hugh all walked out to the hawthorn tree. Underneath it was the largest pot of gold anyone had ever seen. The priest's mouth opened and closed, he rubbed his glasses, then his eyes, then his glasses again. By now neighbours were running over, even the animals were excited.

How. On. Earth? gasped Master Fuller.

With that, John the pedlar of Swaffham told him the story that I have told you.

As much as needed to repair the church, I give it all to you.

The priest yelped: *We could create a new northern aisle, we could have a new steeple. Maybe a bell to call across the fields!*

As he was saying this, something started to happen to Master Fuller. Something started to happen that no one had ever seen. He started to smile. It was a lovely smile, a huge smile that immediately made him look twenty years younger.

It's a miracle!

John ventured a reply.

Well, what it is, is a dream. A dream that became a reality by following its strange instructions, even when it went vague. A dream that has now become big enough for us to live in.

And Master Fuller nodded:

Yes, you're right. Humans make visions, but a dream can come straight from God. Call everyone to the church right now. We must pray and sing and give thanks!

They all came: the blacksmith, the butcher, the weaver, the seamstress, the farmer, the baker, the cowgirl, the midwife—all of them—excited and rejoicing over the news. And once they had prayed and sung, right there in the graveyard, Master Fuller started to dance. The priest hopped from one foot to another like an ecstatic crow, opened his arms and praised his God for sending such a dream.

From that day on, the pedlar of Swaffham was known as John of the Dreams, and for the rest of his long life, on the way to church every Sunday, many would share the way God spoke to them in dreams, even—or especially—Master Fuller.

BE BOLD

Our story of "John the Dreamer" begins with a big dream. The first thing to note is what kind of dream it is. It's not flashy or complex, rather simple and specific. And the pedlar dreams it twice. Every now and then we have a dream that seems to really be telling us something.

Fairy tales always take us to the main issue swiftly, and here it concerns a crumbling church. The place is falling apart, and we get the sense that whatever congregation the priest had is emptying out. At this point there's no overt connection between the dream and the state of the church; that will have to be made in the conscience of John the Dreamer later in the tale. In fact, the priest, Master Fuller, is dismissive of dreams. He seems so distracted by the practicalities of the church's decline he doesn't have time for something so whimsical.

I think Christianity has often forgotten that it is a dream, to its own peril. When threaded to political power it often engenders the will rather than the wonder, the law almost entirely over the spirit. Christianity is a dream in which the very best of us is encouraged to emerge. A dream that challenges and inspires us. A dream in which God speaks directly to us.

It's also worth noticing that John is a pedlar; he comes from humble stock. He comes from a tradition that's said to go back to the Neolithic—the pedlar is the on-foot, cave-to-cave seller of things. John's used to tramping: He's no prince or shining knight; there's no indication he's the sharpest pencil in the pack, but he's prone to these odd dreams now and again. Sometimes it's only the humblest that can walk on divine ground. Even so, there's a lovely, amiable boldness to him.

Of course the priest wants vision. What does that mean? He wants a plan. A big, striplight, daylight constructed plan. A eureka moment. And sometimes God works like that. But sometimes he doesn't. Sometimes a little faith is required. And so humble John sets out.

So sweet it is those first few miles! The sheep in the fields, the waving farmers. Of course, by definition the pedlar would have walked those hedge-flowered lanes his whole life; they are deeply familiar and comforting. But the dream didn't say anything about comfort. By the end of day he's far from what is familiar, the weather's turned rough, and the temperature's dropped. How easy it would be to return home to what he knows.

It can be tough country to leave the known and encounter the new. To remain open and curious, not closed and backward-looking. And all he knows is that the dream centres on a bridge: something that crosses water and gets us from one place to the other. He has to keep moving forward and manage his anxiety. In his own small way, he has said *yes* to the dream, like dear Mary said *yes* to Gabriel. He has picked up the firebird's feather, as they would say in old Russia.

Without the picking up of that feather, the fidelity to that dream, the church will stay crumbling, with no bell ringing across the fields.

And he meets a wild bunch along the way, quite the caravan. Pilgrims, partiers, a beautiful woman with her ticket to heaven (the mind boggles). In other words, he grows in experience, he doesn't just burst into flame the first time he encounters something he's never seen before. In our world this could be a journey over ten years. Our man is getting scuffed by life, broadened a bit. We can all recall the time we first set off on such an adventure and who we met.

Wonderfully, when he finally gets to the bridge he realises he hasn't got a clue what to do. There's no app on his phone, no contact to meet, no nothing. This is when the rubber really hits the road in terms of faith. He just has to submit, to tough it out. This is an odd kind of wilderness vigil.

When he finally meets the shopkeeper, the man both mocks the pedlar and gives him the key to the whole story. *He replaces one dream with another.* I think God does this. This is a very personal moment in the story for me: I realise that's what happened on my 101-day vigil in the Dartmoor forest. I went in with a hunch and was given a much bigger dream to return with, though both hunch and dream come from the same source. I was shown to dig into where I'd been all along.

This is also when the story becomes a circle rather than a straight line—a big part of most myths we remember—Severance, Threshold, *Return*. It turns out that the "Gold Road" that seemed to point to London was actually, in the end, pointing in the opposite direction for John. He has to return to what he knows but *go much deeper.*

Of course when John and Kath dig up the pot under the hawthorn tree, there is writing in Latin they can't decipher. That's when they require the old, serious Master Fuller. He deciphers what they can't, and the second pot of gold is revealed. The senex, the old man, is now in relationship with the dreamer; they are beginning to work together. Without him, they would only have known the first pot. A decent teacher takes us deeper. I resisted this for a long time. I held such a pot for twenty-five years but didn't quite know how to decipher the message.

Now the hawthorn tree is really something. The location of the gold beneath the hawthorn tree is filled with both pagan and Christian symbology alike. The hawthorn is a fairy tree in Ireland, and a place where lovers meet under its blossom. In folklore it is also what made up Christ's crown of thorns. I know of the hawthorn as medicinal, good for blood pressure, and hanging it above your door is a sign of a place that banishes evil. The hawthorn is certainly not a random detail and seems to me a place we would all benefit from digging into. I used to fast under one in Snowdonia, back in the last century.

I am touched by John's conscience at this moment. Much hinges on his relationship to it. A poor man, even mocked by Master Fuller, we would have understood him keeping the gold. But aside from just a little he keeps for his family, he gives it up for the rebuilding of the church. A church that was on the verge of collapse. And his goodness even rehydrates the old priest: He smiles, even starts to dance! I'd love to see more dancing in graveyards. And dancing priests! Suddenly what was stuck now flows, what was depressed now erupts into joy.

As a child, the two great totemic figures in my family life were C. S. Lewis and J. R. R. Tolkien. I think my love of tweeds, pipe smoke, warm, flat beer, and a stroll across the fields comes from their early influence—not that I was supping pints as a toddler, you understand. Warm and imaginative men, they reassured me. They remain pillars of the imagination in my inner Green Chapel. Lewis always said that Christianity was the sun from which he saw everything else.[1] He extracted meaning from its very rays. I feel similarly about myth, and now, wonderfully, the Christian variant, the one he described as "the myth made fact."[2] But it is not quite the time for that story.

What I want to do now is think a little about what kind of words can be used to coax dream eventually to vision. There's a little history squeezed in.

THE VINEYARD OF THE WORD

And as I write, it really *is* snowing. The fire is lit in the library; I have a few puffs of a cigar and peer out the window into the night. There are fast-moving flakes that whirl round the lamppost. I can see a Christmas tree still up in a neighbour's window over the street, glinting gold and red. My own house has changed personality. It's closed in on itself. It's moving towards something like a neighbourly introversion. It scrunches in on itself as the snow falls. I walk downstairs, feed the cats, get the kettle on, work on the fire for ten minutes. No visitors, not much daylight, a little salmon and biscuits to pick on. Mug after mug of strong tea.

And by these words, somehow my imagination has met your imagination and some third thing is happening.

We can be *visioned* both by words spoken and words read.

Plato long ago used to speak of the *esoteric* skill of creative recall and the *exoteric* skill of learning a written text by heart. Nice distinction. This second skill creates opportunity for considered structure and nifty metaphors at just the right moments. One of my favourite thinkers, Ivan Illich, tracks this route in his book on Hugh of St. Victor (1096–1141).[3] Hugh worked out of a monastic community where reading was paramount to the absorption of wisdom, and wisdom was a being—Christ. So to seek wisdom was to seek Christ. What Hugh sought to work on was not just memory but the expansion of his own consciousness.

Most medieval documents were untitled; you cited the first and last line—the *incipit* and its *explicit*. Whatever constituted the first line became the title in the way we would understand it. But fifty years after Hugh, the road from the auditory to silence was well underway, and with it an increased level of authorship. Hugh enabled an oral record, but from then on, writing became the launching point for the accomplishment of the writer's thoughts. As Illich liked to say, Hugh spoke to his students; a hundred years later Thomas Aquinas lectured to them. Hugh's students read his utterances; Aquinas's read his compositions.

By the fourteenth century this level of exegesis provoked such complexity that people started cooking up visual aids to assist in the teaching. Copyists would write out the lecture's outline; soon it was established that to understand the argument you needed the text in front of you. This is an enormous move: writing, no longer to assist sounding patterns but elevated to absolute creative expression.

We should also remember that there was no break between written words—hence you really had to read out loud. When paragraphs appeared, and space around the words, there seemed less imperative to read the words out loud. By now, your ears and my ears were not tuning to a shared thought; it was the individual eye that was now the primary receiver.

THE BUDDING OF A VISION

The place I've witnessed the most dreamlike stories is round the camp-fire of vigilers. Hundreds of times I've gathered by wet wood fires all over Britain to bear witness to what happened out on the hill or in the forest. The four days fast usually has a day and a half either side to locate the spot, go through counselling, and then on the other side to actually speak a little of quite what happened out there. I always advise not to speak of it publicly for at least a year afterwards, though amongst other vigilers it's fine. These things take time to settle, and are not to be passed around like a newborn quite yet.

It's hard to adequately describe the shape of them when they re-turn to camp on the fifth morning. You could say they've *got dreamt*. God did it, the place did it, their empty belly did it, but they are not the same people that wandered off a few days before. And soon they get a chance to slowly work into quite what happened. They get to tell their story, and I listen and then tell it back to them as if it was a fairy tale. The easiest way to try this is to simply begin by putting them into the third person: *Once upon a time, in the middle of their life, a woman walked into a great forest.*

Sometimes dreams are way ahead of us. Sometimes we can glimpse a reality we are far from manifesting, but we get a peek, years ahead of time. I saw little moments of my life now when I was younger, and slavishly worked towards it. I faked it till I maked it, or something like that. One day I woke up, and around me—and most importantly *in* me—were the qualities of things that had imprinted on me years before. But though I recognised the scent, caught the taste in my mouth, I wasn't yet ready to inhabit them. But the glimpse was the thing.

Years ago I taught alongside the groundbreaking psychologist James Hillman. We sat together having lunch, Jim an old man then. He was sick, at the end of his life, but was still a lively dinner companion. He told me about something called the Acorn Theory. That we know, deep down in the subconscious, the oak that we are meant to grow into. He told me of Manolete the great bullfighter being scared to leave his mother's skirts. He felt that Manolete sensed the weight of destiny years before—as a little kid—and was able to submit to it. Hillman said that someone receptive to their intuitions would steer their life according to the skills and circumstances most needed for the acorn to grow.

This wouldn't be entirely conscious, but on reflection you would see an invisible hand guiding you at times towards things you really needed to learn about. He wasn't soft and mushy, Hillman. He looked at me rather like a hawk about to swoop on a rabbit, but then would laugh, and all this light swept out of him.

Back to the fireside.

The fasters' stories have been told, fragile as they often are. They have been honoured, often wept over, the ground of deep feeling has been reached. Then I give them the bad news.

The vigil in the wood was only the second part of a three-part programme. Now they have to return. And most importantly: Now they have to turn their dream into a vision. It's one thing to have an epiphany in the forest, but how do you transmute that to a village wisdom? That's going to take real, solid work. Not very poetic. That takes some work, some nimble-mindedness. It takes more than a hashtag or "living your best life."

The fasters locate something of great worth they lost many years before. It's not a clue to how to get ahead in their career, it's not some wacky insight into increasing their pension pot; it's to do with reconnecting to divine ground. There will be a hundred ways to say it, but that's the thing. In the *Return*, of *Severance, Threshold, Return*, this is the wonder-ground they return to. Almost always with tears, mystification, relief, sometimes regret.

And how does all this help a dream flare up into a vision?

Here's a very famous story from a very famous book. Through symbols it shows us something very grandiose about a future, but then we are going to have to go through a whole heap of trouble to achieve it. It's the story of Joseph in the Underworld of Egypt.

The son of the shepherd was pleased with his coat, loved it. It was lustrous to look at, with long sleeves. Long sleeves meant he wasn't out there with his eleven brothers in the heat and the dirt and the animals. Long sleeves meant his father loved him the most. Long sleeves told him every day that he was special.

When Joseph scurried off to his father to report back on his brothers, they watched and fumed. They saw those sleeves flap cool in the breeze as their own forearms were browned by the sun and scratched by their labours. They felt the energy of their father always turn to Joseph, his eyes always moving quickly over them to rest on his favourite.

He dreamt, the favoured boy, and when he did went swiftly to his brothers.

I dreamt we were in the fields binding up the sheafs and mine stood upright. Your sheafs came and gathered round and bowed down.

Soon he visited them again, this time his father also.

I dreamt of the sun and the moon and eleven stars and they all bowed down before me.

It didn't land well. Even his father was angered by the dream, though he kept turning it over in his mind.

One day on the way to visit his brothers, they saw him coming and a darkness flooded into them. They grabbed him, tore his coat from him, and chucked him into a pit. Rather than killing him they sold him to Ishmaelite traders on their way to Egypt, who then moved him on as a slave.

The brothers, in way over their heads, slaughtered a goat and smeared the blood over Joseph's coat. They brought it to their father Jacob and they let him think his boy was dead. Abject was his soul, and never-ending was his grief; comfortless he was.

Joseph's descent had greater lengths to fall. He ended up in prison, framed by the wife of his owner Potiphar. He may have been a little lofty to his brothers, but surely this was too much punishment? Even in prison, the dreams didn't stay away from Joseph. This time it was as an interpreter for others. There was a servant and a baker of the king, and both had interesting dreams they couldn't figure. Perplexed, they asked him what their dreams meant.

Joseph was wise enough to state that it would be God who showed him the meaning.

The servant described his dream:

I beheld a vine with three branches. The vine budded and blossomed into grapes. In my hand was the cup of Pharaoh, and I pressed the grapes into it and gave it to him.

Joseph had good news:

This is a great dream! The branches are days—it's three days until you are raised up to become Pharaoh's servant again.

At this the baker wanted his dream interpreted, hopes raised:

I was carrying three baskets of bread on my head for Pharaoh, but birds kept taking the bread from the top basket.

This time the news was terrible, but Joseph gave it:

You have three days till Pharaoh takes off your head and hangs you on a tree. It's not bread the birds will be picking, but your flesh.

Not all dreams are ones you want. It takes leadership to deliver news like that and hold your nerve, and Joseph did. He begged one thing of the servant: to petition Pharaoh that he had an innocent man in prison. But when the servant was set free, everything but his free-dom flew from his mind.

For two years Joseph rotted in jail. And yet, so far from what he knew, betrayed by his brothers, betrayed by Potiphar's wife, betrayed by the promise of the servant, he still felt close to God. And even in the belly of the beast, God favoured him. Others seemed to feel and latch onto this closeness. Joseph was trusted.

It was only when Pharaoh himself was troubled by a dream that the servant remembered quite who was down in the depths. The young lad was brought into the presence of Pharaoh. Pharaoh had dreamt of cows emerging from the Nile River, sleek and fat, followed by seven more cows—scrawny and ugly—who gobbled them up. He then dreamt of seven healthy ears of corn growing on a single stalk, then thin ears of corn—scorched by the east wind—swallowing up the healthy. These things troubled the leader.

Quickly shaved and with a new set of clothes, again Joseph said he couldn't interpret the dream himself, but God could do it for him. He told Pharaoh that both dreams had the same message, that the good cows and good corn symbolised seven years of plenty, and the scrawny cows and corn symbolised seven years of famine—a famine so dreadful that no one would be able to remember the good times.

Pharaoh knew in his heart that this was true, and it was God speaking through this lad, so humble and brave before him. His magicians, soothsayers, and diviners had offered none of this clarity. It was providentially clear who Pharaoh should appoint to be in charge of the people and guide them through this crisis.

From being betrayed by his brothers and hurled into a pit, from being forgotten in a cell, Joseph rose up to become a great leader. Over the time of the famine, even his own brothers came back to him, though he didn't recognise them. Like sheafs of corn they bowed down. Like stars in the sky they bowed down.

As Joseph told them years later: *Though you intended evil, God intended something good.*

The man's maturity had caught up with what the dreams knew all those years before.

In the story of Joseph, he's gifted dreams that won't manifest till he's at the completion of the *Severance, Threshold, Return* progression, and, ironically or not, a dream that may have assisted the betrayal by his brothers in its lofty nature. I wonder how Joseph regarded those dreams when down in the bowels of prison. How strange or misguided they must have seemed. Maybe he regretted telling his brothers. But *without* telling his brothers, *without* getting chucked in the pit, he never would have saved the lives of so many in Egypt. The visioning of the dream—what actually made it happen—required a huge amount of sheer living, endurance, and persistence. It needed a sense that God was close, even in the darkest times. In this life there are designs within designs we can't keep up with.

Seems God has plenty of different approaches when it comes to dreams. He offers Solomon anything he could wish for—simple as that—and prudently Solomon chooses wisdom, "a discerning heart."[4] On occasions like these, it seems the dream is more or less a conversation with God rather than anything too symbolic.

Things get more symbolic in the interpretations that Daniel the Wise gives to the king of Babylon. When the king threatens to kill the mystics of his own court for failing to decipher his dreams, Daniel petitions for their lives. Having had the intricacies of the king's dream unravelled in a vision, Daniel then has the confidence to speak to him.

He tells the king of the man himself lying in bed. And it's there he beholds a huge and impressive statue. Its head is gold, chest and arms silver, belly and thighs bronze, and its feet a mixture of iron and clay. This fine thing, this statue that provokes reverence, is then destroyed by a great boulder—a boulder not cut by human hand—that crashes into its feet. The edifice collapses like chaff in the wind. With the statue disassembled, the rock grows into the shape of a mountain, so large it covers the entire earth.

Daniel takes a breath and gives the reading the diviners could not give: that the king himself is the head of gold, but then there will come kingdoms of silver and bronze, then finally a fourth kingdom of iron. Tough and impregnable. But remember the odd mix—the clay as well. It will be a divided kingdom; there will be discord and squabbling, not unification. But God's kingdom is coming, a boulder not cut by human hand. His kingdom will obliterate the others and re-main forever.

A later dream from the king—yes, it's Nebuchadnezzar—was of an enormous and bountiful tree, supporting much life. There were birds in the branches, fruit budding, animals sheltering in its shade. But a divine voice came and demanded it be cut down, trimmed, the fruit scattered. The animals and birds were to flee. But it was not quite total annihilation. The roots and the stump were to be bound up in iron and bronze. And he—whoever *he* is—was to be drenched in the dew of heaven, and would dwell with the wild animals and the plants of the earth for seven years.

What does it mean?

Again Daniel said what needed to be said.

That Nebuchadnezzar himself was the bountiful tree, but it was decreed he was to go amongst the wild things and for seven years give up his role. But all was not entirely over; the bound roots of iron and bronze would herald a return for the king, till he acknowledged that God was God.

And it came to pass.

Nebuchadnezzar was driven from people into the wilderness, where he ate grass like cows, where his nails grew like bird claws, where his hair grew long and uncombed like an eagle's feathers.

And somewhere out in the solitude and under the stars, over seven years, the king came back to his senses and gave deep and humble thanks to his Creator.

It's worth mentioning that a theme we see in the stories of both Joseph and Daniel is a court filled with diviners and astrologers at-tempting to extract information from the night sky. That the heavens weren't a random jumble but a great and finely ordered multiplicity.

C. S. Lewis, writing about a later era—the medieval—said that you could look up into the night and still be reassured, still have a sense of containment. There was shape and reason and information to it.

And it was in the sky that the people viewed their own workings writ large. The spheres transmitted what were called *influences*—the planets affected our psychology, our plants, our minerals. With their night literacy the ancients saw and were confirmed by what they beheld above them. They were contained and in relation. Even theologians claimed that the influence of the spheres was unquestioned, though Christians railed against (1) lucrative astrology; (2) astrological determinism—something that excludes free will: "The wise man will over-rule the stars";[5] and (3) anything that encouraged worship of the planets. But was there wisdom up there? Sure there was. How did the Magi locate Christ?

The mythological commingled with the celestial in the divine naming of the spheres: Saturn, Pluto, and the roaming horde. Whereas now we stare at the unimaginable miles above us, Lewis insists that in the medieval model you would have felt that you were looking *inward*, your inner fates scattered above you.

Some final thoughts. Don't tell the dream what it is: You don't need some dream dictionary. That shoots the bird right out of the sky. How can a book possibly decipher the meaning of something so unique to you? I approach carefully, respectfully. I circle around it. Nail the butterfly to the wheel and it dies. But if I dream of bear I find out about bears. I associate. I study. It may be that I'm working on something—a project—that requires a lot of raw energy, or maybe hibernation, or the protectiveness a mother bear gives her cubs. As Hillman told me, if you tell the snake it's your mother, you've killed the dream. Let it unfold, and over time, like William Stafford's thread, it leads from the fertility of the night to the clarity of day, and both thrive off each other.

Some desert fathers were critical of attention to dreams, and they have a point. But these aren't the kind of dreams they are referring to. Those writings are about vague and ego-boosting reveries that create distance from God and a tendency to self-absorption. But to ignore dreams completely is unbiblical and cuts you off from a kind of inner mythology that is trying to talk to you. Not in the form of spreadsheets and arts council grant applications, but something much more dynamic. But for sure, be discerning. If it floats away, it likely was not worth attending to.

Someone looking at Joseph's dreams could have said they were all youthful ego, couldn't they? But to become what they became involved testing.

In the matter of turning a dream to a vision, know this:

No pressure, no diamond.

You know you have a vision when it doesn't melt away in the daylight.

You know you have a vision when it bumps into obstacles and doesn't go up in smoke.

You know you have a vision when it's robust enough to grow whilst not losing its dreaming roots.

The dream is when we close our eyes and go within.

The vision is when we wake, rub our eyes, and peer out.

11

ON LIMIT

Fog has descended on the mountain, and for days I was confined to my tent. Somewhere out there were four folks fasting, but for now, they and I had to stay put. What had previously been a stunning view of Barmouth estuary snaking and glittering to the Irish Sea was now a sopping wet grey mist. The birds were silent, the wind was hushed, it was hard to orientate. As is often the case, I started to think what William Blake would have to say about the situation. What would he think about such sensual reduction? "The road of excess leads to the palace of wisdom," he used to say. But he'd also suggest, "You never know what is enough unless you know what is more than enough."[1] Push your limits to then discern the frailties of such excess. I strongly suspected that Blake would approve of me sitting in the deprivation of the usual panorama. I think he'd squat next to me, chuckle, and tell me to seek *eternity in a grain of sand.*

There's a story that St. Brigid met a woman who'd been blind since birth. Brigid healed her, and the full glory of this earth was revealed. Tears fell down her cheeks as she beheld the cormorant and the squirrel, the swaying barley, the orchard rosy with apples. But after a time, she wiped her eyes and asked Brigid for a further miracle. That she would be kind enough to blind her again.

I will cherish what I've seen. I will never forget it. But down there in the fertile darkness, with its limit and depth, I was closer to God than I am here. Down there, I could really see.

Brigid kissed the old woman's cheek and answered her prayer.

Limit can be an extraordinary ally. It's limit, not excess, that's a sign of real depth. Understanding limit, appreciating limit, even revelling in it, is an unusual position for an unashamed Romantic to take, but remember I said we need a sprinkling of Duende if the word was to be at all convincing? Let me tell you a story from the Caucasus; I call it "The Spyglass."

There was once a poor hunter who lived with his mother in the mountains. Luckily he had skill with a bow, and most of the time they ate well. But there was a day when nothing came to the hunter, so after a few hours he was growing despondent. He didn't like to see his mother without a good bowl of stew in front of her and a warming fire.

Suddenly he came across an eagle resting on a rock. Resplendent. In a flash he had his arrow out of his quiver and at his bow. But the eagle spoke, in the high and powerful way that eagles do: *Spare my life and I will be useful to you. I will give you a feather from my tail, and if you ever need help, burn it and I will come to you.* An ally like that seemed far more useful than one night's meal, so he accepted the arrangement and walked on.

Soon he came to a goat and prepared to catch it. But the goat spoke, in the trilling vibrato that goats do: *Spare my life and I will be useful to you. I will give you a hair from my beard, and if you ever need help, burn it and I will come to you.* The hunter was wise enough to see that he seemed to be collecting allies not food and accepted the arrangement and walked on. But his gut ached, and he worried about his mother. It was now dark, so he crawled into a hollow tree and spent the night. Deep and strange his dreams. In the morning he walked a long stretch to the sea, hoping for a fish. He waded out into the grey waves, managing to catch a fish that glistened exactly like gold. As he wrenched the fish out of the brine, it spoke, in the gurgling and watery way that fish do: *Spare my life and I will be useful to you. I will give you a golden scale from my skin, and if you ever need help, burn it and I will come to you.*

Though wobbly with fatigue, the hunter recognised that something marvellous was happening, and he placed the fish back in the salty swirl and accepted the scale. Shivering, and running up and down the beach to dry off, he spotted a red fox just up shore, and again he creaked back his bow, though now half expecting the next scene, as the fox spoke, in the amused and cackling way they do: *Spare my life and I will be useful to you. I will give you some fur from my tail, and if you ever need help, burn it and I will come to you.* So tired he could only nod, the hunter accepted the fur and the fox darted off into the brush.

For the rest of the day the hunter walked; no birds, no animals, grey skies, chill under his cloak. He came to a settlement and visited a little hut on its edge, smoke rising from the chimney. Inside was the smallest, oldest woman he had ever seen. Wrinkled like a currant she was, squatted down by the fire, stroking her belly, gazing up and clearly hungry. The hunter immediately reached into his pocket and gave her a coin. A smile spread across the bannocked moon of her face, and she scuttled off to buy some meat. Later they ate well, and the hunter felt finally refreshed, but he could feel the old woman was disguising some sorrow. So he enquired.

At first she didn't want to disturb his eating, but after some gentle nudging she spoke to her distress, let it hover in the air between them. She told him the kingdom had a harsh ruler with many magics. That he had an odd entrancement on his daughter. That he had given her a spyglass that could see every single thing in the world. With this device you could receive information in a fraction of a second. Any man who would want to marry her had to be nimble enough to evade her sight three times. You showed your pedigree by disappearing. By becoming nothing. With the spyglass at her disposal, it was next to impossible for any suitor. Any man who failed was slaughtered. So far ninety-nine young men had died, including both the old woman's sons—her winners-of-bread, her right arm, her sustenance.

Of course the next day the hunter made his way to the ruler's compound. He was astonished at its opulence, the servants, the gathered wealth. He said he accepted the challenge, but on one condition: that he was allowed to hide not three times but four. It is something to negotiate under that kind of pressure, but the daughter accepted, whilst reminding him: *Your head is hanging by a thread!* Next morning, when the sun had barely opened his great hot eye, the hunter slipped away from the compound and burnt the eagle feather. Instantly the eagle was there, picked him up, and carried the hunter to his nest, higher than the cloud line. He then spent the day covering the hunter with his wings.

Well, it was a hard thing for the daughter to locate. She worked over all the usual spots men hid in, and he wasn't there: not down a well, in the tavern, under his mother's apron, in an empty promise, not even in a hollow tree. Finally she spotted just a couple of hairs from the fur brim of his hat under the eagle's wing and shouted: *I found him! He did better than the rest, but I found him!* Next morning, when the sun was just starting to stir and contemplate the day's labours, the hunter slipped away from the compound and burnt the hair from the goat's beard. Instantly the goat was there, and the wild old thing carried the hunter to the very edge of the known and unknown world, dug a hole, nudged him in, and spent the day covering the hole with her furry, ample body. Well, it was a hard thing for the daughter to locate. She had almost given up, almost started to gaze up behind the planets, when she spotted a little cloth from his jacket under the girth of the goat's belly and shouted: *I found him! He did better than the rest, but I found him!*

Next morning, when the sun was stifling a yawn and assembling his rays, the hunter slipped away from the compound and burnt the golden scale of the fish. Instantly the fish was there, and the sea spirit placed the hunter in the mouth of a pike and took him far out over the green daggers of the sea, then deep down into its depths. Well, it was a hard thing for the daughter to locate. She gazed on desert, swamp, forest, and meadow, and he was simply gone. She despaired until her mother petitioned her to scan the deep sea. After some hours she saw the pike open its mouth to swallow a fish, and she saw, tucked down inside, the face of the hunter, and shouted: *I found him! He did better than the rest, but I found him!*

There was excitement in the chief's compound now as they felt the trap tightening on the hunter, but also some barely whispered admiration for how far the hunter had managed to stretch the affair, his skills under pressure. Next morning, when the sun was deciding to place one warm finger slow and curly over the top of eastern hills, the hunter slipped away from the compound and burnt the fox's fur. Instantly the fox was there, and told him to relax and take a nap under a tree, that he'd fix everything. The fox then dug an underground tunnel to right underneath the daughter's chambers, halting just a few feet under her. Try as she might, wherever she aimed her spyglass, she couldn't find the hunter. Never would she think to look under her own feet. That night when they met, she was so exasperated she asked for an extra day to locate him. With an easy smile he agreed, and the next morning he burrowed along the tunnel and again spent the day right under her feet.

As dusk came, she flung the spyglass against the wall in frustration, and suddenly a familial darkness flew out the window with it. Some healing had come. Overnight her father slinked away into the forest, and the hunter became the husband of the queen of the kingdom. It was a merry time, and the hunter's mother was called over to the wedding. She danced for three hours, then three hours more. Contentment, for just as long as is proper, ruled the house.

LIMIT, MY TEACHER

I've been hearing that technology is Luciferic my whole life. Not from my parents, but it's a long-standing idea that reemerges every few decades. It may be that there's more of a case now than I would have considered in my youth. Back then it was evangelical comic books that used to tell us that multinational corporations were run by satanic cults and that the world was only four thousand years old. I can be forgiven for not hanging my soul on such opinions.

But there's an unease now, and it's growing in me. As a parent, as a Christian, as a human. I know from rueful experience that something is happening to my attention levels since having a smartphone. I know how flimsy my focus seems to ten years ago. I know that—if I don't measure it—these little machines pour endlessly into my retinas impulses and distractions that really don't have my best interests at heart. I know screens are corroding something in me. Something meant for something better.

As we explored earlier in the book, for many kids, porn is now the entry point to erotic experience. Not a glimpse of burlesque, but hard-core pornography. Something that grabs their fledgling imagination and imprisons it, and oddly, *sedates it*, makes it smaller. Cookie-cutter scenarios. Your physical longings are not growing in tandem with a particular girl you may glimpse in science class, but stretched on the rack of whatever can be thought up next. There's no Dionysus, no Aphrodite, no Krishna, no Song of Songs, no Troubadours, no Van Morrison *Moondance*—that's all done with. The old singers of love in the court of Eleanor of Aquitaine knew of *amor*, not just eros, and delayed erotic gratification was a place of simmering, imaginative delight. Some of the greatest poems of any age got written within that place of longing. The strange result of endless access to the abyss of porn is a generation of young men who struggle to maintain erections. Viagra at twenty-two. That tells us something profound. That at the core of a man's visible sexual expression, right down at the base, something is saying:

This isn't right. This isn't actually what I want.

"The Spyglass" is such an extraordinary story. The fact that the one place where the spyglass can't find you is right underneath the princess's feet. To conquer the spyglass you have to disappear. In a time of frantic visibility, in a time of social media trending and hashtag madness, true sovereignty is defined by your capacity to be untrackable by the secular world. Yeshua is the clink-on-the-link to a world not as mired and erratic and inflamed as one sold us endlessly on the screens. The fact that the hunter has a healthy relationship to nature and animal allies is not lost on me either.

So how do I disappear?

Be smoke. Unpredictable. Unbuyable. Hold yourself to a higher account.

I would suggest that the one place the spyglass can't see is the prayer mat directly underneath you. It may be an awful long time since you've knelt down and prayed, but maybe you should try it. It may turn out to be one of most appropriate positions to take in this world. The one really important yoga move they forgot to tell you about.

Tracking the West for many millennia has been a dark spirit; these days it's disguised as a lifestyle. It's had many forms. The thing it wishes for most profoundly is that you forget that prayer mat. Once you've forgotten that, it has you entirely.

If there really is—on a granular level—something intrinsically Tower-of-Babel-esque wicked about screens, can I suggest we form a sort of pushback of beauty against them? If you use them, make sure you do some good with them. Donate to charity, ring a suffering friend, study a course in Classics Literature or the like. Turn something attempting to become a deity back into a tool again. Work it on *your* terms not its. Make a covenant with limit. And if that doesn't work, smash it with a hammer. You'll feel an awful lot better.

Limit is an instructor I've struggled with my whole life. One who I only realise in middle age is offering invitation not imposition. Limit doesn't have to lead to a thin-lipped denial of the world, but actually a sense of relief and even relish for a discerning ground of absorption. Don't be flailed alive daily by the news; pay attention to what's happening on your block or in your village. It's OK not to have an opinion on everything happening in far-off climes. It doesn't mean you're stupid. It means the opposite. It means you may have something approximating conventional blood pressure; it may mean there's a big old part of you that is simply not for sale. It's worth practicing a little unavailability to the world's carousel.

Maybe we should have fewer friends and cherish the remaining more. Maybe we should read fewer books but linger longer with them. Maybe we should check our twitchiness for *more*.

It's *moreness* that seems to be behind the human contribution to climatic change.

For much of my adult life I've harboured ill will towards the Christian relationship to ecology. Or what I thought it was. I saw it as a collection of old white guys stroking their beards and making horrible judgements on nature, and, circling out, making proclamations on women, Indigenous cultures, even their own bodies. And, sadly, there are elements of history where that can be located as fact. Millions of people have a similar reaction, and don't overthink it. They can plonk Christianity in a drawer marked "Bad colonial attitudes we'd rather forget," and back they go to their Gong Shower.

It will come as no surprise to you that I am a fan of kinship with nature and know that is a beautiful possibility through a Christian lens. I'm still critical of some Christian legacy in this regard, and the reported missionary abuses are enough to have me running off into the forest and never coming back. But I can't do that. I have to stick with the trouble. I'm with Reverend Everett Pesonen, who, back in 1945, said we should listen to "the voice of the salmon."[2] If developers only perceived water as inanimate and sterile, then before too long it would be. The salmon that return to my bend in the Dart River are fewer and fewer these days.

The Christian emphasis on humans' specialness can—and has—provoked a Lords of Everything complex. As Tom Hayden reminds us, we measure everything by Gross National Product, which is not a spirit that pays much attention to the disappearance of species, especially the tiny critters.[3] Even the notion of being a steward—a slight demotion from a Lord of Everything—can still bugger everything up. Again Hayden notes that if my precious Dartmoor salmon disappear, they can be engineered in hatcheries. But lacking genetic diversity—there are a million problems there too. We corral, farm, and growth hormone the crapola out of the earth and wonder why it's not working well for us. Surely the instructions of Genesis work well if we're all in the Garden with God, but gets steadily messier once we're into the Fall, and doing our own thing, cranking up our sense of ourselves as little gods. *I don't think we should be stewarding anything at all once we've fallen out of right relationship with the sacred.* And that's much of what the Genesis myth is: an incredible picture of right relationship and what happens when that gets murky. As has been stated before, it would have been great if the Ten Commandments had something to say about pollution.

I don't think the earth thinks and feels like humans do, but I also don't think it is dead matter to do with what we want. It has informed and moved and challenged me my whole life. I think the earth and its denizens are fantastic and mysterious and oddly porous. There are a few things the Bible doesn't talk much about, but it doesn't mean such things aren't present.

The earth is filled with intelligence. Not in a human type of way, but in its own grunting, creaking, fluttering, crowing, slow-evolving, lightning-fast type of way. If you listen closely for a long time, it's talking to us. It may be telling us about heaven.

The Orthodox thinker Elizabeth Theokritoff poses the question: Does Christian Tradition begin with the belief that the creation is "very good" and "the earth is the Lord's," or is it existing for man and his "dominion"?[4] I think we know. Theokritoff then starts to lay out some of the earliest Christian ideas about this.

She points out that Christianity is the only great monotheistic religion where God actually enters creation to be part of it. In other words, has a dog in the race. Christianity arrives in a Platonic landscape where the body is a husk around a soul, imperfect and soon to be shrugged off. For some pagans, the Christian notion of a resurrected body was distinctly odd, especially as there was no reincarnation or possibility of floating off somewhere more etheric. In the next life you still had a body, just not that one that slowly became dust.

Christians loved God, loved each other, loved sex, loved nature. And in all of that the body was something to happily thump, scratch, and be hugely thankful for. The body is not a tomb, it's a pleasure, and it goes where we go because we're completely bound up with it. This has got horribly confused down the centuries. St. John of Chrysostom remarks that it's not that the body is foreign to us, but rather death and decay.[5]

Theokritoff sensibly suggests that it's impossible for us to be able to say a great deal about how a restored cosmos or resurrected body may appear (that's rather beyond our ken), but "the significance of this organic relationship (with the beyond-human) is not that it links us with what is mortal and perishable; rather, that it links earth and everything belonging to it with what is *imperishable*, since the nature of earth's human offspring has been taken up by God himself."[6] That's worth combing over a couple of times. That by God electing to live a man's life, and dying as a man, this means we are now connected to the life beyond this one.

I'd put it this way: *We are being prepared for eternity every time we behold beauty.*

We can't crucify beauty without steadily walking into hell.

Every time we walk the dog we are surrounded by hints of the Kingdom of Heaven. That's a big thought to swim into. One of the ways we can practice being saintly is to notice that grace. And the more we abide in it the more folks around us start to notice. This is one of the attributes that used to define saints; you glimpse more of the Kingdom of Heaven around them. They are literally an eye-opener. A saint has had the saliva and dirt of the great druid Yeshua wipe the blindness from their eye. They behold.

Another quality of a saint is a reduced tension around them. A force field. There's a wonderful story of Paul of Obnora, the Russian hermit who lived within a lime tree for three years. A visitor found him covered in birds, sat next to a bear, foxes, and rabbits. There was none of the usual drama between species. I wouldn't immediately try and befriend a bear, but you could begin with a bird? A saint is some-one deep in theosis; they are like a smoky lamp being cleaned, so the divine light really starts to shine out. In this sense they are icons, a wonderful thing is radiating through them. They are clear, not murky in ambiguity. A saint emanates what Theokritoff names "the author-ity of love."[7]

The rural saints lived in a world teeming with animal intelli-gences: bustling up against the furry, the scaled, the winged, and the wild. Whilst nature provided all sorts for human beings' benefit, that benefit was not meant for greed and avarice, but to provide endless and varied mirrors of the Creator's wisdom. A huge and happy web, a luminous patterning. Everything is talking to us.

There's also the beautiful image that the Holy Spirit once inhab-ited a dove. That for a moment at least there is an avian dimension to the trinity. And to signify such a moment as the baptism of Yeshua by the wild desert man John the Forerunner. Wild man, Christ, and Holy Bird, all in the same radiant moment. In Mark I. Wallace's book *When God Was a Bird*, he really takes this image for an awfully long walk. Longer than the associations may warrant, but he has some provocative thoughts. Most of the references describe the Spirit coming down "*like*" a dove, but John states, "I saw the Spirit come down from heaven *as* a dove and remain on him."[8] It's a subtle but very important distinction for Wallace's argument. Of course, God appears in burning bushes and speaks from thunder clouds; it's not new for him to communicate through his beloved creation.

Wallace is an advocate of the idea that the root position of Christianity is actually animism, something that will have a few reaching for the smelling salts. Why? Well, simply put, it allows consciousness to everything. Everything is alive in the way that it is. It's been a rather dismissive term in the West, a rather academic phrase for the religions of many Indigenous cultures. At best it's been a little nostalgic, at worse little short of a slur. Nonetheless, most of us sort of "get it" as a phrase. And not only do we get it, giving reverence and sacredness to the wider earth seems an awfully sane thing to do in a time of climate emergency. It is in fact the lack of that that has contributed to the ecological suicide bid we seem to be in.

A Christian take on it could be to honour and even pray to the radiance that exudes through nature, but not the tree, creek, or mountain alone of itself. Wonderful though they may be, they are not of themselves to be worshipped. That is different to some pagan traditions. But nature is *infused*. If the Holy Spirit can exist in a bird when he feels like it, then it stands to reason that all of nature, God's *it-is-good* creation, can be a vehicle for the divine. The proviso is to worship the Creator not the creation. Adore, protect, relish in the thousand-fold creations of the artist's hand, but follow where they lead, not as a devotional end entirely in themselves. The Christian perspective is described well by Metropolitan Kallistos as "through the creation to the Creator."[9]

Back to the notion of the Bird-Spirit. Wallace quotes scripture:

"In the beginning, God created the heavens and the earth. The earth was formless and void and darkness covered the waters. And the Spirit of God (*ruach Elohim*) hovered over the face of the deep" (Genesis 1:1–2).[10] The *ruach Elohim* Wallace alerts us to is grammatically feminine, with a feminine verb form that describes the movement of the Spirit *merahefet*, which he claims translates as "sweep over," "flutter over," "hover over." Even as poetry rather than literalism, he's making the point that the winged associations are there right at the beginning. He's aware that his wider thesis doesn't chime with God's condemnation of Israel when they worshipped the Golden Calf, and the horrific consequences that followed, consequences that ensured an extremely soft, soft approach to any animal-god associations from that moment on.

I have sat quietly in nature more times than I could ever count. It is and always was for me bristling with stories. As a Christian I've come to believe there's a creator that's both independent of the earth (even the whole universe), but also infused within it. Rather like getting the best of both worlds. When I became Orthodox I found there was even a word for it: *panentheism*.

It means "all in God," that God is both within creation and outside the universe. Everything exists in God, it's not just that God exists in everything. This is such a massive thought we can only grasp at it. But I can look at the whorls of my finger, the fur of a badger, the melt of a snowflake on a blade of grass and get a glimpse. I make my gaze smaller not bigger, and funnily enough something happens. I think there would be a huge amount of good medicinal care distributed if we Christians started to actually look carefully around us again, instead of bunching our eyes shut and sheltering entirely in abstractions. That's not an unbiblical suggestion.

Back on the mountain, that sacred fog eventually cleared, and I was allowed the almost indecent grandeur of a view I had previously taken for granted. I sat with my jaw dropped. For a moment I had *morning-has-broken* eyes to it all, and I was absolutely silenced, tears as large as berries falling down my cheeks. A day later the vigilers would return, eyes shining, and story after story of their time immersed in what one called *Merlin's breath*. Suddenly we were laughing and crying and wondering at the audacity of such invitation to limit.

12

ON EVIL

I once dreamt of an angel at the bottom of my bed. I would have been about eight. He seemed absolutely beautiful. He would have appeared almost human had his pupils not been red. He sat there and spoke to me quietly, said he'd noticed me, singled me out, wanted to be friends. I remember a kind of perfume in the air. He sensed I was scared, and that flattery wouldn't work whilst I was this anxious. So he told me he was going to leave but I could always call on him, though it was not quite time to know his real name. He said I never need be alone, and that he would always, always be close by. And with that he was gone.

I woke and I had wet the bed. That was no angel I would ever want to meet again.

You don't get grown without encountering darkness. You don't get grown by assuming everything has your best interest at heart. You don't get grown without experiencing peril. At some point, you're going to meet the Devil. All over this earth, in all sorts of cultures and mythologies, you're going to hear of seriously unpleasant, seductive, charismatic energies that are looking to sow division, disillusion, and addiction into your waking hours.

No storyteller anywhere would tell you evil doesn't exist. One of the reasons we tell myths is that we can better apprehend it and give artfulness to its tricks and manoeuvres. Grow wise to it. No tribal initiation would be all honey and kind words; at some point you would wrestle darkness.

The writer Jeffrey Burton Russell would suggest diabology has a slightly more forensic grip in the Latin West than in either the Islamic or Eastern Orthodox world.[1] It seems there aren't really images of the Devil before the sixth century, though by then a rich iconic tradition had been established. Of course, in the Desert Father stories we are provided with all sorts of stark and diabolic spirits.

To the Byzantines, the Devil was never an independent power source but a being crafted by God. Profoundly fallen, but a creature made by God. Evil can't come from God, but from a *privation* of God, an unlovely, phantomlike nastiness. The Devil is a being that endlessly turns from its essential nature, which is good. The Devil in us is that part that has turned the farthest from God. That's where it rests. The old idea is the Devil doesn't force us to sin, but he derives great pleasure from tempting us. If he forced us to sin, the sin would lose the frisson that comes from it being free will.

In medieval Christianity the image of the Devil grows simpler, more impactful, terrifying, while in folklore of the same era he's often ludicrous, sometimes impudent, a bit of a buffoon. So he's evoked either to keep you in line or to let off some tension, like an Inuit Trickster story. Anything from the pagan world with horns is fair game, so Pan (from the Greek south) and Cernunnos (from the Celtic north) unfortunately get lobbed into the emerging, drawn-with-one-line Devil. Wiggling within the shape are all sorts of more minor players and also titles: *Belial, Lucifer, Morning Star, Satan, Beelzebub*, and associations with pig, wolf, crow, dragon, eagle, snake, bat, monkey, and on and on. But even with all that variety and dynamic range, the Devil tends to be perceived as ultimately one being.

Because pagan associations were made with the Devil, the places that pagans loved were often viewed with terror or suspicion. A cave, a grove, a bend in the river, even the edge of a field could have good village folk quaking. Mercifully this nature-wary attitude is less apparent in the early Irish Christianity, where a far more positive, even playful perception of the wild is noted. Whilst not worshipping a hill or rowan, a monk could sit in contemplative bliss and bear witness to the holiness that radiated *through* it, a kind of electrical pulse from the Creator.

I've been lucky in my own life to spend well over a thousand nights under canvas or stars. I've been alone in big, dark deep forests. Not once, not one single time have I ever experienced anything like these descriptions of the Devil. These places can be profoundly mysterious, wyrdly charged, but evil as a wandering, intentioned presence is not something I've encountered. Nor have I met anyone who has. That doesn't mean I haven't experienced wickedness in my life or view it as something of entirely human construction. I don't. But I'm baffled by folks who have not even spent a night in the bush and claim it as the Devil's playground. They don't always know what they're talking about.

I have a caveat: that there are always places that are taboo. We get this throughout the Indigenous as well as the Western world, places that are simply not for humans. Tribal people sense this and avoid them. Not necessarily bad but simply not for *us*. They are mystery places, thin zones. That's not what I'm getting at. It's suspicion, even abhorrence of the earth that I'm disturbed by.

So here comes *Gentleman Jack, Old Horny, Old Scratch*, to get us locking our doors and saying our prayers. The Devil seems very granular most of the time, more likely to be present in discord within a family than hovering horned by the bedside, but I'd be foolish to discount the possibility. I'm one of those signs and wonders folks, after all.

For real horror we've now replaced the Devil with Hitler and Hell with Auschwitz. We've seen in real time what the Luciferic feels like when it pours into this world through a dark idea, egoic possession, a turn away from goodness. The old mythologies of the sulphatic man seem almost quaint when confronted with what we know of paedophile priests, sex trafficking, blood diamonds, and war horror. Of course, literally none of these horrors are new. Evil is evil is evil, but the sketch we give of its shape continually contorts and develops, moves from a charcoal line to pixelation. But is evil really so easy to spot?

The examples I give are straightforward to revile, but I'm left thinking about the more insidious influences. What's threaded through Big Pharma, some Silicon Valley companies, even some people's obsession with leaving our planet for Mars rather than being accountable for the mess. This is tough to write about. There are pills I take every day that I'm grateful for. It's hard to even approach these areas without coming across like you want to form an Amish community. But it's these complex threads that both aid and abet where I'm most aware of angels and demons slogging it out, and the trouble with discerning quite what's at root. Gives with the one hand, seems to take away with the other.

The old Pannish Devil gets to smile, put on his hat (over the horns), shrug his shoulders, and announce he's been retired, whilst dissolving into the hardwiring of ten billion smartphones. Almost impossible to locate, with all the good also being done on such devices. Becomes too much hard work to try and discern the difference. Better just go with the flow, man.

I'm walking a terribly thin line here. I carry a phone in my pocket and am both thrilled with the contact it allows me with my loved ones and appalled at its fizzing away of my imagination, hooked as I can be on its ever buzzing and beeping displays of distraction, and with root ingredients of its creation gathered by little more than slaves in the most dreadful of conditions. In *Parzival*, the Fisher King's wound is briefly tended to by precious minerals mined from places that can ill afford it. What wound are we attempting to salve by endless distraction? Distraction that can lead to isolation and withdrawal. And in fairy tales, those are always the optimum conditions that create maleficent influence. The nasty old man in the black hat always gets you on the lonely walk home from the fair.

I'm sceptical of many overviews that map the right and wrongness of things. I'm old and gnarly enough to know of the myriad of grey and the competing claims for truth that abound. But—and it's a big *but*—I also growingly feel that discernment, even vigilance, is the only sane approach. I can't swill around in whatever influence is rag-dolling me at the time. That's the Odyssean island of the Lotus-Eaters. I don't think devilment has remotely vanished. But it's pulled off a big trick: The old image of the Devil seems to have dissolved into abstractions, and it may be far easier to do its work there. An ancient idea is that the Devil will be most successfully hidden in what seems to be a no-brainer good thing for everyone. Of course, following this train of thought can make us completely neurotic. But there's nothing abstract about evil when encountered.

I think many artists would concur with the notion that anything that messes with their intuitive talent would have a root in the diabolic. This is the kind of position that William Blake would have held. Blake's extraordinary world has no interest in reason as a guide to anything at all, so quite what he means by God and the Devil is a moveable feast. As a painter I can go a long way with Blake, but I can't hang my soul on him; I need my final Teacher for that. I love much art, but I don't worship it or regard it as perennially for the good. It is what it is. There are few safe havens, that's for sure. The Devil's rocked up in the pews of church enough times and in the mouths of some earth-hating, women-hating, life-hating preachers to know that we have to address the influence on a case-by-case basis. A church can be a far more perilous seat than an oak grove.

There was a lad I once knew whose father threw himself under a tube train on the London Underground. The travesty of that violence opened a hole in my friend's head. He experienced too much darkness, too early. Years later we played in a band together. From a distance his life seemed almost blessed: money, chart success, acclaim. From a distance he had an irresistible kind of glamour. But his muse got steadily darker, the drugs got heavier; it was as if the whole atmosphere around him had changed. The angel at the bottom of the bed had residence.

By the time it was all about black magic, crack, and S&M clubs, I knew this was a ride I most definitely needed to get off. We shared a bottle of whisky one night, watching Minneapolis rockers The Jayhawks. Sitting on the steps of the West London venue, I told him I had to get out, leave the band—my sheer health depended on it. For a second the darkness seemed to clear and he peered thoughtfully at me:

If this life isn't any good for you, do you think it's good for me?

It was a real question, and being a kid, I fudged it. Of course *no* was the answer. It was eating him from the inside, the life we had. Alienated from our manager, agents, publishers, the sourness of our attitude was all we had to lean back on. Rock 'n' roll. I gave a few platitudes about everyone finding their own way in life, and then shuffled to the exit door as fast as I could. I couldn't bear to be around him anymore, and he knew it. I felt the perfumed angel nearby, and it was simply too disturbing.

So I quite deliberately lost touch with him. I knew things had gotten worse. Jail time for drug dealing, endless cycles of rehab, terrifying weight loss, restraining orders put on him. For twenty years I stayed well clear.

One day, I knew I had the strength to contact him. I sent a note to a very old email, simply stating everything I had admired about him. His lyrical ability, his literary tastes, his general artfulness in the face of nineties Britain. I suddenly, in a rush, remembered how great he once was. I got it all down, wrote the note, pressed *send*.

Nothing.

For nine months, nothing.

Then one afternoon, contact. A long letter arrived. A letter he claimed he had been preparing to write for the last decade. Astonishingly, it was an apology. For all of it. He had ensured that leaving the band was a kind of slow-drip financial torture at a moment when I had nothing. He owned this. He went further, describing the glee he'd felt in doing so, and the remorse he now felt. And in the depths of his prison experience, he slowly, almost agonizingly, began to come into contact with what he called a Higher Power. A light of some kind.

Cleaving to this feeling, my friend began to crawl from his Underworld towards something edifying. The man who wrote this letter, so battered by experience, was nonetheless out of hell. His big moment had been surrender, a handing over, to the presence he was now connected to. He ended the note:

God bless.

I've read it many times, this letter. When he died of natural causes a few years later, even more so. He had stayed clean, started to write again, had a girlfriend and a cat, loved to go out and catch the sunset on the Thames River, just like he did when we were teenagers. His heart had recovered enough, his soul healed enough to find a simplicity he once scoffed at. Now he cherished it. He defied the overwhelming narrative that Old Scratch had mapped out for him. It was a miracle, and something I could never have foreseen.

I've been reading Peter Shaffer's play *Equus* from back in the seventies, and many of these issues swirl around in its pages.[2] The play hinges on a bad thing, a terrible thing, an evil thing. A teenage boy, Alan Strang, is found to have blinded six horses with a spike, all in one night. The job of a psychiatrist, Martin Dysart, is to decipher the psyche of the young boy, and "fix" him.

But Dysart gets upended in a way he could never have anticipated. In the very normalizing of the boy, he starts to suspect he may be fighting evil with evil. He dreams of being a priest back in Homeric Greece, sacrificing a herd of children to some dreadful, hungry deity called the Normal:

> The Normal is the good smile in a child's eyes—alright. It is also the dead stare in a million adults . . . it is also the Ordinary made beautiful; it is also the Average made lethal . . . my compassion is honest . . . but also, beyond question—I have cut from them parts of individuality repugnant to this God, in both his aspects. Parts sacred to rarer and more wonderful Gods.[3]

Gradually the story of that night in the stable assembles itself: an encounter with his father in the audience of a blue movie, an attempted deflowering by a young woman, and the strange Horse God he calls Equus filling his mind at the crucial moment: "When I shut my eyes, I saw Him at once . . . I couldn't feel her flesh at all!"[4]

Terrible though the event is, Dysart can't help but track Strang's devotion as a form of worship in a world devoid of friends, culture, and filled with TV jingles: "He lives *one hour* every three weeks—howling in a mist."[5] Dysart resents, deep down, castrating the lad's form of worship, terrible though it may be. This being, a shrink who hasn't given his wife so much as a peck on the cheek for six years, and gets in touch with the wild by heavily insured, prepackaged, packed-lunch trips to the Med, whilst *"he* stands in the dark for an hour, sucking the sweat off his God's hairy cheek!"[6]

The *explicit* evil of the blinding meets the *tacit* evil of the God of Normal. Part of the play's genius is that it doesn't overlabour this, just walks us further and further into the complexity of the story. In the way we've been thinking about it, seems like Old Nick has this play in a kind of pincer move. The magnetic tug between the raw dark of the stable abomination and the isolation and banality of what surrounds the lad has him struck like a trembling bell.

You push a log underwater, up it floats. You rob us of our worship, be careful what surges in to fill the gap. I think Blake would be very hostile indeed to many aspects of the God of Normal. Extreme blandness will always incite its opposite, and maybe in terrible, vivid fashion. Suddenly the Devil is not rocking up with hooves and tail, but in a beige and benign guise, nodding understandingly.

There's often what's described as metaphysical evil and natural evil. Natural evil you see in a tsunami or an illness; metaphysical is a swirling world of usually invisible spirits creating all sorts of misery and encouraging very bad decisions. Natural evil is a no-brainer, but over the last few hundred years metaphysical evil has waxed and waned as a publicly condoned reality. Could it be, to use Jeffrey Burton Russell's phrase, that "Satan has expired" in imaginative and intellectual discourse?[7] That after the witch hunts, and the thinking of Locke, Descartes, and Spinoza, Kant or Voltaire, we simply couldn't stomach evoking the Devil so overtly? We'd got him out of our system. There are endless exceptions to this but a paper trail for sure.

Of course, when he's no longer taken seriously as having metaphysical existence Old Horny can be demoted to a symbol and then get a new lease of energy in literature and the arts, most famously in Goethe's *Faust*, a work that just about straddles both Enlightenment and Romanticism. A bit like Blake, Goethe isn't trying to transmit one particular meaning or point, but offers a safari into his own head, and by default something of the culture's concerns at that time. Russell again: "The shift from the Devil as theological person to the Devil as literary personage was permanently fixed by Goethe."[8]

There's a dizzying array of names I could now add to the conversation around evil and the notion of the Devil: Nietzsche, Dostoyevsky, Twain, Freud, Jung, on and on. My little sketch here is not about the reality of wickedness but how the historic notion of the Devil turns and twists, ducks out of sight and reemerges. The Devil, as far as I can tell, is holding on to transpersonal atrocity as well as localized human corruption—that's what makes him the Devil. A nuclear war benefits absolutely no one (I'm paraphrasing Russell here) and yet all sorts of energies buffer along the way to its potentiality, and the kind of mental health stresses that such possibility offers. I sense there is a vast unknowable dimension that moves through our lives, and I would suggest our mandate is to attend to the grace in that dimension.

A way to push back at the Devil.

Loving attention.

Go for a walk to a wild place. Go for a drive to your grandkids' house. Go for a hike up a hill and look up at the stars. Find something and really look at it. Open some hidden chamber of your heart to it and give it twelve secret names. Praise it, be generous to it, be specific to it. A baby's face, a procession of ants, the Plough, a book that needs kissing it's so darn good. You'll know it when you see it. Be a praise maker. The Devil hates this kind of thing.

HATE IS THE SATAN OF LOVE

I'm going to draw on some central ideas in the book *Reviving Old Scratch* by Richard Beck. It's a very intelligent read, clearly aimed at Christians who no longer regard the Devil as a *thing* but a symbol, not an entity but an image. He pushes against that without getting too didactic. Beck leads Bible study in a maximum-security prison, and that gives his ideas a much-needed, well-trialed grit. He also claims that Satan (from the Hebrew meaning *ha satan*, "adversary") can be seen as much as a *relationship* as a person. Anything that is getting in the way of you being part of the kingdom of God is a satan. Here's his list:

> Hate is the satan of love.
> Exclusion is the satan of inclusion.
> Oppression is the satan of justice.
> Tearing down is the satan of building up.
> Competition is the satan of cooperation.
> Revenge is the satan of mercy.
> Harm is the satan of care.
> Hostility is the satan of reconciliation.[9]

That's useful to me, "a relationship as much as a person."

Beck also brings up Thomas Jefferson's Bible. Jefferson—almost as a prophet of modernity—made his own cut-and-paste version of the Gospels. He cut out all the weird stuff. We get Yeshua as a trimmed-down moral teacher, friend to sinners but far less about Jesus "doing good and healing all who were under the power of the devil, because God was with him."[10] Many just don't want to think about the supernatural stuff, or see it all as entirely symbolic.

But Yeshua was an exorcist. It's not a subtext, it's front and centre. Exorcism literally kicks off his ministry.[11] From Yeshua's temptations in the desert, it's *war* between Christ and the Devil, played out in market squares and villages and wherever Christ heals. And when the Devil roosts in the heart of Judas, it looks like game over. Out there on Skull Hill people saw the King of the Jews die. Scratch won. But rocks get rolled away, Sunday comes, and the most astonishing aikido move in the history of creation: the mind-melting, soul-joying return of the Lord of Hosts.

Whilst Christ didn't much encourage rebellion against the Romans, he was in all-out assault against that which was adversarial to his Father. We think we are too sophisticated for the notion of possession and exorcisms these days. That those things belong to another age. Take that attitude outside the first world and see what you find.

Beck uses an example of the *banality of evil*, a phrase that comes from the writer Hannah Arendt.[12] When Arendt, a Jewish political philosopher, got to meet the Nazi war criminal Adolf Eichmann, she was almost disappointed by what she experienced. That he was less Grendel and more party clown. That he had unthinkingly followed orders. And it's that unthinking obedience that she saw as the ordinary face of evil. No one is foaming at the mouth or bellowing in

Latin, but just quietly "getting on with it." And in that "getting on with it" they are a satan in the face of love.

Yeshua is countercultural to the world. The pattern of this world is often frantic power grabs, and then he starts telling us that anyone who wants to be first must be the very last and the servant of all, that he himself came not to be served but to serve—y'know, blessed are the meek. It's this kind of thinking that kept me away from him for fifty years. Too exacting, too weirdly dangerous. This is not Achilles energy.

From the world's perspective this is outlaw talk. It doesn't make sense. It's not workable. The world really doesn't operate like that. Well maybe it *doesn't*, if Old Nick, Old Scratch is the prince of it. But we should hardly be taking our cues from that compromised, survival-of-the-fittest, to-the-victor-the-spoils kind of mentality. Spiritual warfare for me is to turn away from the magnetism of that over-whelming narrative, though at times it seems to be the very oxygen we're breathing, the very water we're swimming in. I'm trying to get, dare I say it, more conscious.

Do I spend more time with demons than I do angels? Certain ideas have a restorative, regenerative, rehydrating quality to them; others pull us away from our friends into dark corners and gossip queasy conspiracies. Angelic and demonic atmospheres both. Environments that provoke both the best and worst of us. I'm going to attend to where I'm hanging out, both in my own mind and out there in the world.

This doesn't mean only wearing beige, distrusting the wild, becoming fearful not curious of the earth. This doesn't mean avoiding what Lorca called *Duende*, that gritty, chomped-up understanding of where eros and melancholy lightning-crash into each other like an old woman's final flamenco dance. It doesn't mean not loving the wild

darkness. Not at all. Is his last years Johnny Cash very much regarded himself as a Christian, but remained, mercifully, the Man in
Black. And who's more badass than Yeshua? Eating the unripe burden of the earth as a catastrophically beautiful act of love. As the civil
rights activist Bayard Rustin put it, we could get involved in "angelic
troublemaking" and subvert the world with love. It may sound woo-
woo but I think it's all we've got.[13]

When I was a kid, it was the Devil that had all the energy. Like a
magnet I floated towards. I was floating away as fast as I could from
Bee Gees Jesus. The Devil was all leather jackets and rebellion and
sexy danger and riding the red horse of desire all the way over the
edge of the cliff. He's had the most astonishing PR. God (which is
still a word I have almost no feeling for) floated about remotely somewhere in space, but you may actually meet the Devil, standing smok-
ing by the jukebox, or out by the crossroads at midnight. You can see
how much twentieth-century propaganda I must have absorbed. He
lived in Elvis's quiff, Jim Morrison's leather trousers, Keith Rich-
ards's battered telecaster. I don't see it like that anymore. He's no
longer the poster boy for cool. He is unutterable darkness.

I see him in the pool cues of the Hells Angels beating the lad to
death at the Stones gig at Altamont, rejoicing at the women's domestic violence shelter down the road in Plymouth, cheering on the cops
as they *I-Can't-Breathe* George Floyd, seeding pure-nastiness in the
war in Ukraine, cracking the champagne at every turn from good in
every cramped little household from Galway to Sydney. Every time
there's division and hatred of Otherness, there he is. He's not cool,
he's a vile, ingenious prick. And part of that genius is that he can
appear in the guise of one of his most famous names, Lucifer—*Angel
of Light*. Keep sniffing for sulphur, keep testing the spirits of our age.

I must tell you that I dreamt again. Not of the angel, but where he comes from. I was taken to a place where prayers no longer worked. And the landscape I stood in got darker and darker and darker. Dark containing a vibration of despair I have never experienced as a human. There were no fires, no pitchforks, nothing so theatrical. It was profoundly awful. A description simply can't do justice to describe how it felt to be in the absence of Light.

This is not about trying to convince you the Devil is a prowling-about, embodied phenomenon. You will have your own take on that. But I wanted to circle around the atmosphere of this character and his works. Despite the wonder of the earth and the grace many try to cleave to, there are levels of suffering and darkness so grotesque it leaves us speechless and sometimes broken. The Galilee Druid saw this reality and fought against it every chance he had. Christ says *resist*. Yeshua seems to push against two particular enchantments: passivity and disconnection. They seem to be royal roads for Old Scratch. Lotus-Eaters and existential dread, one feeding the other. Rage against the dying of the Light. Stand up for beauty.

The Adversary has stalked the lives of humans for an awfully long time. Traditionally the way we have kept his chaos from the gates is with a vivid display of what the writer Keith Thomas called "ecclesiastical counter-magic."[14] We have used speech, sacred drama, liturgy, and vigil to banish darkness from the community. As Christians we mock such things at our peril. We are ceremony people, story people, poetic people. We are *writ large*, and we regulate fear by creative acts of display and imagination.

When the Anglican Church abandoned holy water, the sign of the cross, and the sheer richness of image the Catholics possessed, it replaced them with a rather stark agenda—prayer in cold pews and the thin cry for repentance. They had little symbology sufficiently florid to root the concerns of the public, many of whom were caught up with all sorts of magical combats with neighbours and enemies. There was no longer *ecclesiastical counter-magic* to protect the congregation from their neighbours. To those out in the lonely fen and isolated moors, this was a disaster. They required a greater vivacity to their psychic battling. The vacuum left by the departing medieval saints was swiftly occupied by the wise women and cunning men of the Tudor countryside. A conjurer of the time, Robert Allen, happily wandered the lanes with the audacious title "God of Norfolk."

The English spirit, for millennia fed by ornate mythologies, may have just about been able to tolerate Catholicism with its pantheon of saints and angels, but when it was so diligently pruned, when the magical thinking of the people was given such heavy penalty, then the church inadvertently opened a back door to animism.

Sir Thomas More was known to complain, "In such wise witches, have many fools more faith a great deal than in God."[15] God's inscrutable visage peering down on the chilly-pewed churchgoer was less compelling than the attentive ear and the healing poultice of a hedge woman. In time, relentless promotion concerning the values of hard work and prayer would pay dividends, and this older form of magical bartering would be regarded as primitive. Even so, it has never quite died out completely.

A development was that new magical formulas rubbed embarrassingly close to particular Roman Catholic creeds and Latin paternosters. In response, the church made the argument that to rely too heavily on prayer was tantamount to superstition, and one should seek natural cures before supernatural ones. Speedily heading to the wizard's home with a case of gout was off-limits. Of course, the irony is that the herbs contained in many suggested cures could not be more natural—and who created the herbs in the first place?

Things got crazier. Some reverends went with the trend. Robert

Burton furiously scribbled: "Poor country vicars are driven to turn mountebanks, quacksalvers, empirics."[16] The Devonian parson Hugh Atwell acquired a delicate reputation as a magician because his prayers actually seemed to work. Another cleric, John Bell, was caught attempting to cure fevers by writing words on paper and giving them to anxious parishioners, and the Reverend Joseph Harrison went down for the "charming of pigs."[17]

This hands-on approach slipped under the royal nose and was found in the healing work of five-year-old Richard Gilbert from the green hills of Somerset. Gilbert was revered as beginning his practice as a "stroker" when he was but one day old. As a slightly older infant healer, he would gather the infirm on a Monday and set about their swellings and general discomfort. When asked about his powers, the little cherub would whisper: "I touch; God heals."[18] Another practice was to hoist up sufferers of wasting diseases to grasp the still-twitching hand of a freshly hung villain.

The upsurge of popularity for edge magic coincided with the wider tide of Neoplatonism that swept through Europe at that time. A clear invoking of the old pagan worldview—that the world was not dead matter but animate and open to communication—made the seemingly "mad" descriptions of potential cures less crazy, even in the minds of England's intellectuals. It was a world beset less by evil than by an absence of light, a world soul of immense sophistication intertwined with the inner life of all. This road of thought, initiated largely by the Greek Ammonius but brought to fullness in the work of a Roman, Plotinus, has had a profound impact on the thinking and cultural life of the West: From its revival through Nicholas of Cusa and then the Italian Marsilio Ficino, it roared a trail in the minds of Blake, Hegel, Wordsworth, Keats, and Jung.

The more Christianity jettisons its wyrd, nervously polls for popularity, abandons its saints and delicious eccentricities, the more it opens the door to pasty-faced New Age woo-woo. Because underneath such appeal is the longing for the kind of truths Christianity has always embodied. We should hold our nerve, and also not be naïve about the time we are entering. And to name that time clearly we could turn to myth.

In Russian fairy tales we hear the phrase *Moving from the Horse to the Wolf.* I think we live in the Age of the Wolf, but we still think we can potter along on the old nag. In the story "Ivan and the Grey Wolf," Ivan's horse is consumed by a wolf that erupts out of the trees. Ivan loves his horse—it was given to him by his father; it's a thoroughbred.

As Ivan stares in horror at the gobbling up of his horse, the wolf tells him that to achieve what he needs the boy must jump on *his* back. No ornate saddle, no warm companionship—rather, grabbing the fur of this utterly wild creature and holding on for dear life. With his old life in bits around him, Ivan makes the right move. He sniffs the wind and realises there's no returning. The wolf will go stranger routes, push him into danger on occasion so he grows deeper. The wolf is just as beloved to God as the horse is.

Sometimes when the wind from the desert comes, we refuse the deepening it offers. Of course we do. We won't climb the back of the wolf, but pine for the steady footfall of the horse. It may be that Ivan sat for seven days like Job grieving his old life, but in the end he clambered onto the new.

The wolf's not sentimental but awesome. When I say we live in the Age of the Wolf, that's not throwing shade at the wolf. It's not implying he's wicked. I'm saying we *need* him. It's only from riding the wolf that we negotiate the blizzard of our times. The horse, bless its steps, is still too domestic. Job's house—maybe like ours, maybe like much of Christianity—has been blown over; it's wolf-wisdom or nothing at this stage. I believe it's what I'd call Initiatory Christianity with all that ecclesiastical counter-magic that the wolf will remind us of. There's a wisdom to gathering it back in.

13

ON PRAISE MAKING

And where has all this wrestling led us?

It leads us, finally, to praise.

Praise is the natural expression of a life tuned to the mythic. This can be in the way you weave a Brixham fishing net, nurture a garden, attend to learning a poem by heart. These examples may seem slight, but they're not. This capacity of leaning into beauty, of a sustained gaze to the good even in the face of a concentration camp, gulag, or prison, can be the difference between life and death. Praise is most effective in its specificity; it's not to be dished out in great, sugary heaps. Praise is a response to a movement of the heart. These responses can't be placed in a line and expected to behave. That's more like a generic affirmation than praise, and real praise has at its heart a blessing. When delivered with integrity praise makes connections, warms the cockles, opens possibility.

Praise is an extraordinary discipline in a world of *me-first*. Especially when it's noting a quality that you yourself would love to have.

Having to take a breath, a humbling, before you give praise is an even deeper expression of its gifting. Praise can be a decision as much as an instinct. It can take practice. It's not naïve or simplistic to give praise—it reveals largeness of character. It shows that you're a grown-up, not trafficking in sarcasm and nasty little digs. Praise properly delivered strengthens rather than sedates. A storyteller should move the energy in a room in a particular direction: through duress and challenge to finally wonder. The words of a teller are an attempt to make the barley stand straighter in the field, the salmon leap higher in the river. Praise carries news of the universe with it, procures little green shoots from the largest of ash piles. It is a radical art; it changes lives and is absolutely free.

Inability to praise is a sign that you're not quite grown, that there's damage to your wingtips. It may be that you've not received much of it yourself. If that's the case you have to do what the poet Rumi suggests: "If you haven't been fed, become bread."[1] Even if it feels difficult at first, try to distribute the protein denied you. And, over time, something of a miracle can happen. It returns to you. Reality softens, you notice far more of the good in people and circumstance, you may even notice a little of that good in yourself. Praise can cause that nasty little inner critic that continually berates you as a fraud to lose its clawlike grip on your shoulder. Generosity is infectious; it changes everything around you if you are really paying attention. Praise is a royal road to the kind of wealth Wallace Black Elk would have understood. Be careful with criticism, maybe take a minute before you let fly. Where in you is it coming from? To critique can be vital, absolutely valid—Christ did it constantly—but as mere mortals we often attack simply as an expression of various unattended wounds. In our assaults we grow smaller and smaller, the light dims, and our affection is petty and conditional.

One of the elements to praise making is fidelity, and that's hard in a society addicted to severance. We're not anywhere long enough to actually praise in an earned and convincing way. We are used to upping sticks, cutting off, breaking ties in a way that would have seemed dangerous and certainly rash to previous generations. We bolt at the first sign of trouble. In my twenties I was proud of the fact that I'd lived in fourteen different parts of Britain. I styled this behaviour as a kind of gypsy spirit. It wasn't anything of the kind. I was a scatterling, not a traveller. I was on the run from something. I was on the run from the noble and ordinary obligations that mark someone else as being indebted to a place. I didn't want that, so I floated. The price was quite literally a rootlessness, a difficulty in striking up meaningful friendships; I didn't know what it meant to be claimed by a place. I was all hat and no cattle at this point, all sizzle and no steak.

When I say *claimed* I'm making a distinction between being of and from a place. You can be *from* a place and have no real knowledge of its ecosystem, history, cultural weight—you just scoot from A to B. To be from a place has staleness of vision attached. You've rather tuned it out due to overfamiliarity. There're millions in this position. This creates a mindset where you no longer cherish the idiosyncrasies that make up your little corner of the earth. The things you identify with are the same things that unite people everywhere these days—we all want the same phone, sneakers, insurance. We no longer have any sense of the hedgerow gossip or the patterning of stories that mean we can tell the myth of a place back to itself. Make your place blush. Be loyal to the bells of your village, I say. To do that, we have to trade a little growth for depth, we have to be more reluctant to sever.

Now to be *of* a place is to be claimed by a place. You may not even have that much choice in the matter, barring a certain openness of character. It may not be where the bones of your dead are, maybe not be the place you were raised. But you submit to the claiming by the quality of attention you give the land. Underneath the motorway that roars past your house is a road, and under that road is a path for horses, and under that path is a track for donkeys, and under that track are long grasses wet with dew, and in the dew are the hoof-prints of a doe. Track some of the practical history and innate poetry of the place that has claimed you.

And what would that claiming feel like? You get a feeling that you want to stay. That you're prepared to pay the toll of being ordinary to stay. The toll of repetition. To keep showing up in some fashion. Give something back. Whether it's a smallholding or helping out in a community library on a day off or the homeless shelter, get down into the mud of things. Roll up your sleeves. Get to know what's be-spoke about your place, that's not like the next town along. At some point you will realise that you're no longer floating.

I've realised over the years that we are heavily defended against an experience of our own beauty. Now what defines beauty is a whole other book, but I'm certainly addressing a kind that we rarely see on social media. It's to do with presence not persona. It's to do with something essential not ornamental. It's not to do with more stuff. When I was younger I couldn't discern between my desires and my longings; I can now. Desire is satisfied every time a parcel of books drops through my door, often within a day of ordering. Desire is sat-isfied every time I wander through a mall and slip into any number of fast-food restaurants. Desire is satisfied when I settle for porn over intimacy. The gap between desire and delivery gets less and less and less. In the West, most of us live in a time of feasting and very little fasting.

And then I realise. I'm *not* satisfied. And I'm more and more impatient with any kind of wait at all. Then I immediately want something else. I'm hooked on the whole wave of desire and delivery, but actually any deeper satisfaction grows less and less. I wave my spoon like a high-chair tyrant.

Longing isn't the above. Longing is something many religious traditions understand. In myth what you long for is rarely what you receive. However, you'll receive *something*, and it may be even deeper than the yearning. Longing has a quality that isn't locked into what Christianity calls the *passions*, that habitual field of lusts, wants, and envy. It sees through it, whilst establishing a disciplined falling into the mind of God. We fall in over and over again, and sometimes we fall out. Then we dust ourselves down and again discern the difference between desire and longing. Even the saints did this. A praise maker sings of what they long for, not just what they desire. The Troubadours would have understood this very well.

When it comes to getting claimed, when it comes to understanding longing, we—as I've written before in this book—make a covenant with limit. To do that places us at odds with much of what is around us these days. Learning how to say *no* has enormous spiritual strength attached to it.

A praise maker would understand both the pastoral and the prophetic. You would have at hand tools that affirm both the dignity of the known and the freshness of the unknown. They would dwell in the tension of both tradition and innovation. As a storyteller there are stories to tell at a funeral that bring everyone together, and stories to tell in a town hall meeting when we have grown complacent in what we think we know. When we are stuck we need to be startled. A praise maker always uses specific not general terms. No blandishments.

Blessings not affirmations. Look, really look, at what it is you're addressing. Endless, unfocused encouragement can have a numbing effect.

We are being fed counterfeit directives much of the time these days. At least for a life that seeks more soul, more grit, simply more imagination at its core. Less content, fewer screens, less online presence, not more. This is hardly news, but I must persist. I repeat, pay attention to the eccentric, the specific, even the irrational. Get to know the prayer mat underneath your feet—it's the only job left in town for you. Most of it is mirage.

A praise maker has discernment on what they praise. A perilous wound is not a ritual cut. An addiction to disorder in your private life is not an indication of initiatory grit. In an adolescent culture, discernment is the first thing to take a hit. We start to think perpetual drama is somehow prompting us to wisdom. Maybe not the case. Maybe if there was any wisdom present, we wouldn't eternally be caught in such exhausting theatre. Give your attention to the grace. The quality of attention we give elevates that thing, can make it holy in our eyes, so we should work on our discernment and choose carefully. No more jabbing our pen in our wound and calling it art. In myth, any voyage into the Underworld involves you bringing back beauty. If there's no beauty—no gift—then you've actually not reemerged, no matter how much you claim that you have. There's a great deal of this going on.

Don't be afraid of quiet. Don't be afraid of solitude. The saints are cheering you on, remember, so we're never that alone anyway. We get weakened if everything is expressed all the time. The tyranny of disclosure. Christianity in the evangelical West is rather extroverted, and that doesn't suit everyone. It can feel like it's on steroids. An in-breath is quite all right; we're not betraying the Great Commission.

There's no still small voice if we're bellowing our opinions at every party we get invited to. Maybe turn a few invites down. An old teacher once told me the next time you see a woman at a party you'd love to get away from her boyfriend, leave and go live in a cabin for three months. There's something your soul wants to say to you that just temporarily showed up in her face. But you don't need to literalise the impulse for union. Save everyone some trouble and be quiet for a while.

Praise makers speak what I call a blue feather language. This observation comes from my interest in magpies. They appear black and white, but when you keenly observe their feathers, you'll notice the occasional blue. When an argument is walloping about between two polemics, some subtlety is bidding to announce itself. As I've mentioned, it's like making a third way from the impulses of two wild horses, or dwelling in the tension of the opposites, abiding in the bone house, handling Keats's "negative capability."[2] This isn't a wishy-washy or centrist position, but a display of some imaginative nimbleness. And it doesn't mean you can't be decisive when the moment calls for that.

Getting made involves understanding two things at once: Things end and miracles happen. It's naïve to assume either can be influenced except by the divine. Climate emergency is a very real thing, but it would be unbecoming of me not to cleave to the grace, the unexpected, the miraculous. It's a matter of style. Because we struggle with grieving we don't know how to collectively approach the thought that this will all end, and because we are cynical we don't know how to stay open to magical surprises. We cover all of this up with a thin, yellowed trail of sarcasm and a click for our next purchase. We're really damaged in this way.

Somehow, underneath, we know this.

I think the West's self-esteem is lower than we may suppose. Despite empire—or likely because of empire, technology, and the rest—I wonder about the stories we tell ourselves in private. Many feel they have fallen out of a story that used to nurture them; others believe they are still in a story but it's become a nightmare.

We have to start telling different stories. Stories we'd want our kids to live in. Every time I tell a story, I ask the audience—*Shall we go?* And they hopefully bellow back, *Let's go!* Such is their yearning for a great tale. We need new ways to tell the greatest story of all.

It's no good to go chasing after meaning as an abstraction; meaning comes in the *doing* of things. Meaning comes in how we reach out towards the universe, with our Underworld limp and our capacity to let barley grow in our words. There are robbers stealing the horses of your imagination: Kick them out. This book has been full of hints as to how to do that. If I'm too explicit you will be left with a pamphlet not a story.

In the end, I say to my students that the myths we remember come down to three things:

What do I love?

What'll it cost?

What am I prepared to pay?

Wallace Black Elk showed me what I loved, on that rainy hillside in Wales. I swooned into it, and lost friendships, career advantages, and what seemed occasionally like my reason. I think I paid what it cost in full. I am changed and I am different. Much of what I have gained I offer to you in this book. Getting made, becoming a real human being—well, it's a lifetime's work. But I have tools and calloused hands, and I'm waving them at you right now. Let's raise our visor to the beauty of the world again.

Epilogue

———•◦•———

ON THE ANCIENT GOOD

A praise maker is well on their way to becoming a saint. The writer Elizabeth Rees states, "The term 'saint' simply meant someone wise and holy, or any good Christian who had died."[1]

Well, I don't know if you are holy, and hopefully not dead yet, but I bet somewhere knocking about there's a bit of wisdom. Saints weren't a big part of my life growing up. I remember when my uncle Bryan died, at the funeral he was described as a saint, and I didn't know what to think. I thought saints practically floated; I didn't think they had an allotment and a fondness for tandems. Now, I wonder. Bryan made you feel different about life when you were around him (which is a saintly thing to do); he endlessly taught by example—the last hours of his life were spent with family singing hymns around him. As John Moriarty would say, Bryan was a "singing Christian."[2] Sinless, no; saintly, maybe.

Maybe, just maybe, we could try that ourselves. This may be

where I have been quietly walking us these last chapters. If you're still reading, please dig in for a little while longer.

I wonder if we could very respectfully "scuff up" the word *saint* again, plant a few flowers in it, occasionally reach in the darkness for it, rather than discounting it as something absolutely otherworldly.

To cleave to grace, to not be battered by the hypnosis of so much social media, to get to know a patch of land, to get to know yourself, your animals, your people, seems an eminently sensible thing to do. To get to know your God. When the Druids wanted to know something, they *limited* their views rather than *expanding* them. If they couldn't read the moment through one square foot of earth, then there wasn't much to know. Blake would have understood.

Time in the bush is not abdication, or fantasia, or some bonkers fringe activity. It can be a moment to place your fingers in the wound of Christ and doubt no more. It can be a waking up, not an enchantment. As I've said till my voice is hoarse:

Reverie leads to participation.

Brigid knew this, Catherine of Egypt knew this, Petroc knew this, the two thousand saints of Bardsey Island most likely knew this. You can be a saint in training: with your wellies and your sandwiches and your Marches of Witness and your Extinction Rebellions and your smallholdings and your storytelling and your alms-giving and your food bank and your bag of apples for the freezing Dartmoor ponies in the middle of the night. Feel your way. Think your way. Dream your way. Try not to do it all on your own—that can get very muddling.

My other caveat as a wilderness guide is that enormous periods of solitude are not for everyone. It's a nice idea, but most of us need a human face at some point in the week. As the Lakota Sioux say, there can sometimes be "too much Great Spirit."[3] I have to flag that up. You may find what you need sitting quietly under a tree in a park twenty minutes a day. That's not a cop-out.

The God of the Christians was a scandal from beginning to end. He was born a fugitive and died an outlaw, and then had the audacity to come back. He is the most countercultural God of them all. The bravest, the strangest, the most mystical. Don't go anywhere near him if you want your life to stay just-so.

Become a saint.

It won't surprise you that I have a story about that.

This is a tale that wrapped itself around me when my home burnt to the ground.

It would have been the middle of the night when I heard the sound. Even in the depths of a winter slumber I knew what it was. I lurched like a thunderous bear from my furs and blankets, ran to the door of my tent, and gazed out. The crash of collapsing tipi poles was what had roused me. My other tent—of two I lived in—was on fire.

It was an awful drama watching the flames eviscerate everything I had so lovingly placed in that large, yellowed, and weather-worn tipi. Love letters, antique chests, piles of books, Persian rugs, cords of rope, camel bags stuffed with clothes, lumps of turquoise, a natty collection of hats—everything was pulverised by flame. In some mad moment of fleeting courage, I slipped between the columns of fire and grabbed my grandfather's military sword, buckled and burning hot, and lobbed it into the dark grasses. I crouched, despairing, and surveyed—still only half awake—this odd Viking burial of a scene. Utterly alone on the side of an ancient English hill I cried my heart out.

As grey light shambled in I could see the damage. There would be no salvage operation. Ashes, almost everything was ashes. My own face was covered in floaty bits of the stuff. I looked like a grief-stricken badger. I can only guess that a spark from the open fire lodged in one of my jaunty piles of blankets and simmered there unseen for several hours. At some ordained moment it flared up. The tent I generally lived in was far more mundane than this one—this tipi served as a chapel to me. I prayed in there, sat quietly in there, brought everything that seemed beautiful to me and laid it there. All of that was gone now, all of that was ashes now. I combed through the ashes with a rake so it took order, ensuring there were no embers left. I then turned back and walked into the remaining tent, where a sickness claimed me for several days.

In the time that followed, I drifted in and out of this story whenever I was strong enough to turn a page. Over time it would consume me so utterly I would write a book on it, tell it in lecture halls, longhouses, nightclubs, theatres, and under canvas all over the world. It has never let me down. It's the medieval tale of the Arthurian knight, *Parzival.* And I hand it to you now, with all its disasters, triumphs, giddy and sobering truths. Let it, like all the stories gathered here, warm you, nourish you, and lead you home. Let it lead to recovery.

⸺ ◦●◦ ⸺

There was once a boy who grew up in a forest. He didn't know he was the son of a king; he knew nothing but birds and badgers and the rain on leaves. For the most part he was happy. He lived in a settlement with his mother and a few servants. She'd once been the queen of Wales, but after the death of her husband on the Bagdad Road she retreated to the woods. She wanted her son protected from notions of chivalry and crusades. She wished a long life for him. However, after meeting three knights of Camelot one day, he elected to leave and become a knight. In an attempt to get him returned safely, she dressed him as a fool and whispered contrary advice in his ear. As he left on a donkey she fell dead to the forest floor. That part of his life was over, though he didn't know it.

Over the years the lad was educated in different ways: by encounters with women, a disastrous first experience of Camelot, a mentorship by an older knight, a marriage. It was in his marriage bed he started to hear his mother's voice calling to him, over and over. Not realising she was dead, he set out to retrace his steps to where his life began. Late one afternoon he came across a lake in a large, brooding forest. On the lake was an angler fishing, an older man with a hat with peacock feathers protruding out. He invited the young man, whose name was Parzival, to dine with him that evening. He gave directions and resumed his fishing in the gloom.

Parzival ascended higher up tracks that got smaller and twistier. Wolves howled, bears crashed at a distance, and a heavy fog descended. He was relieved when he beheld the towers of an ornate castle at the very top of the mountain. That night at supper he realised that the angler king was wounded to the groin and in some considerable discomfort. His mentor knight had always advised him not to ask questions, so he stayed tight-lipped, even as the evening became stranger and stranger. A lance that bled was brought into the hall, and a grail that when placed produced as much food and drink as anyone could eat. When even this could not produce a murmur, the pain-riven king produced a sword forged in heaven as a gift. Still nothing.

In the morning the castle was empty, as if no one had ever been there. Though relieved to leave, Parzival was left with the terrible sensation that some enormous opportunity had just passed him by. Over the following days he was reunited with many of the figures he had encountered in his earlier life. It became abundantly clear that his silence was a catastrophic error. That the king's wound was the earth's wound, and everything would stay absolutely fallen until the young man re-found Wild Mountain. Unable even to return to his wife, riven with shame, he endlessly retraced his steps, but with no success. Many years passed like this, and the land languished in decline. At night the mountain haunted his dreams: majestic, haunting, and always just out of reach.

How do we find by will something we were once gifted by grace?

One day he was led by pilgrims to a hermit's cave, and it was there he met a holy man who knew plenty of the Grail Castle. Indeed the hermit was the brother of the wounded king and knew exactly the story of Parzival. Finally Parzival was given the terrible news that his mother was dead; in fact, many of the characters he'd encountered over the years were relatives, even an uncle whose armour he'd taken after he killed him. Over fourteen days, the deep secrets of the Grail were revealed to him. Finally weathered enough to receive such news, Parzival wept with remorse and asked for forgiveness.

It was as much a hermit as a warrior that left the cell of the holy man. He was a simpler, humbler man, contrite in his way. Though the sage had told him he'd never find Wild Mountain again, he persisted, but in a new way. He surrendered. It was no longer only effort that would take him there, but God's grace. Christ took his reins.

It was in this state he was received back into the Round Table, and given the extraordinary news that the way to Wild Mountain was now clear. The being giving him the news was no tonsured priest but Cundrie—she the supreme defender of the Grail. With Cundrie and his half brother, a warrior mottled black and white like a magpie, they made their way back to the angler king. With no effort, no battle, no bravado, there it was. The forest and the small track winding up and up. The great, noble, untrammelled shape of the mountain.

It was like before but not like before.

There was the king and soon the procession of the bleeding lance and Grail. Candles were lit and guests craned forward in the torched darkness to hear if Parzival would respond. The man knelt slowly by the Grail King and asked, with infinite tenderness:

Uncle what ails you?

The change was immediate. Flush came to cheek, glint to eye, firmness to grip. He was healed. And as he was healed, so was the land. Salmon leapt higher in the stream, barley straightened in the field, a crow's wing was unwrapped from the sun, and all bathed in its life.

The sweet, simple, hard-earned hymn of a question unlocked the deepest pain.

Over time Parzival would become the keeper of the Grail.

It was like before, but not like before.

What has changed?

Everything. Where once Parzival saw, now he beheld. The devastating simplicity of the response—no magical formula or cryptic koan—is like the Christ of Mark's gospel. His compassion is absolute, shamanic in its efficacy. Some long for greater floridity at that moment, but in that request reveal how little they understand about what's actually going on. It is a different reality Parzival now occupies, where once was rock and tree now is *the kingdom*. This is a beatitudinal state, and it's taken every bit of Parzival's journey to get there. Consciousness is like that. He could have had the question whispered in his ear by his mother at the beginning of the story and it wouldn't have done any good. He needed the wasteland as much as he needed Camelot. The question has to come from the prayer that is revolving endlessly in the den of his heart. Until he's speaking from there, it's all mud, smoke, and darkness. These things can't be said with effect until they're known, and God has his timing for that.

How do we find by will something we were once gifted by grace?

We can't. We simply can't, and we're heading to an existential crack-up if we think we can. But we can take heart from the fairy tales and note that certain opportunities of the soul come around more than once. And that we can ready ourselves, deepen ourselves, humble ourselves. We have Christ's full attention—let's not waste it.

In the end, it's surrender to that loving attention that will get us home.

Gather your thrown-away stories, get made, stand firm on occasion, and attend to the grace. That's what makes a real human. To be a praise maker is to behold His earth in this way. Practice and grace are connected. Some of us may feel too old, too jaded, too sullied by the world.

Well, as the tail of this book prepares to run into the mouth of its beginning, I say *hogwash.*

Rumours tell of a Wild Mountain. To be of service to the Ancient Good.

Don't let a chance like this go by.

Notes

Introduction

1. W. B. Yeats, "The Magi," *Selected Poetry* (Macmillan, 1968).
2. John 16:13 (English Standard Version).

Chapter 2: On Bones

1. Genesis 2:7.

Chapter 3: On Initiation

1. 1 Corinthians 3:2.

Chapter 5: On Passivity

1. John Lee, *The Half-Lived Life: Overcoming Passivity and Rediscovering Your Authentic Self* (Globe Pequot Press, 2011), 5.

Chapter 6: On Passion

1. Bernard of Clairvaux, *Selected Works* (HarperCollins, 2005).
2. Teresa of Avila, attributed to, but not found in collected writings.
3. Martin Shaw, "Eager as a Young Moon: Hymn to Inanna," author's own telling.
4. Erik Varden, *Chastity: Reconciliation of the Senses* (Bloomsbury Continuum, 2023).

5. Federico García Lorca, *In Search of Duende* (New Directions, 2010).

6. Martin Shaw, "King Henry," author's own telling.

7. Antonio Machado, *Times Alone: Selected Poems of Antonio Machado*, trans. Robert Bly (Wesleyan University Press, 1983), 57.

8. C. S. Lewis, *The Four Loves* (Collins, 2012).

9. Ted Hughes, *Winter Pollen: Occasional Prose*, ed. William Scammell (Faber and Faber, 1995), 239.

10. Søren Kierkegaard, quoted in Charles K. Bellinger, *The Genealogy of Violence: Reflections on Creation* (Oxford University Press, 2001).

11. Arthur Rimbaud, *A Season in Hell* (Independently published, 2016).

Chapter 7: On Prayer

1. John Moriarty, *A Hut at the Edge of the Village*, ed. Martin Shaw (Lilliput Press, 2021).

2. Rowan Williams, *Passions of the Soul* (Bloomsbury Continuum, 2024), 23.

3. Philip Zaleski and Carol Zaleski, *Prayer: A History* (Houghton Mifflin Harcourt, 2005), 56.

4. Alan Kreider, *The Patient Ferment of the Early Church: The Improbable Rise of Christianity in the Roman Empire* (Baker Academic, 2016).

5. Mark 9:29.

6. Luke 22:42.

7. John Chrysostom, quoted in Sister Juliet Jennifer, *The Prayers, Quotes and Sayings of Saint John Chrysostom* (Kindle Edition, 2016).

8. St. John of Kronstadt, *My Life in Christ: The Spiritual Journals of St John of Kronstadt*, part 1 (Printshop of St. Job of Pochaev, 2015).

9. John Moriarty, *A Hut at the Edge of the Village*, ed. Martin Shaw (Lilliput Press, 2021).

Chapter 8: On Guilt

1. Patrick Kavanagh, *Collected Poems* (Penguin Modern Classics, 2005).

2. Ibid.

3. Marie-Louise von Franz, *The Feminine in Fairy Tales* (Shambhala, 1993), 130.

Chapter 9: On Envy

1. Marie-Louise von Franz, *Shadow and Evil in Fairy Tales* (Shambhala, 1995), 218.
2. Antonio Machado, *Times Alone: Selected Poems of Antonio Machado*, trans. Robert Bly (Wesleyan University Press, 1983), 147.

Chapter 10: On Dream

1. C. S. Lewis, "They Asked for a Paper," in *Is Theology Poetry?* (Geoffrey Bless, 1962), 164–65.
2. C. S. Lewis, *God in the Dock: Essays on Theology and Ethics* (William B. Eerdmans Publishing Company, 1994), 54.
3. Ivan Illich, *In the Vineyard of the Text* (University of Chicago Press, 1996), 42.
4. 1 Kings 3:9.
5. C. S. Lewis, *The Discarded Image* (Cambridge University Press, 1964), 104.

Chapter 11: On Limit

1. William Blake, "Proverbs of Hell," in *The Complete Poetry and Prose of William Blake*, ed. David V. Erdman (Vintage Books, 1988), 35, 37.
2. Reverend Everett Pesonen, quoted in Tom Hayden, *The Lost Gospel of the Earth* (Sierra Club Books, 1996).
3. Tom Hayden, *The Lost Gospel of the Earth* (Sierra Club Books, 1996), 55.
4. Elizabeth Theokritoff, *Living in God's Creation: Orthodox Perspectives on Ecology* (St Vladimir's Seminary Press, 2009), 74.
5. John Chrysostom, quoted in Sister Juliet Jennifer, *The Prayers, Quotes and Sayings of Saint John Chrysostom* (Kindle Edition, 2016).
6. Elizabeth Theokritoff, *Living in God's Creation: Orthodox Perspectives on Ecology* (St Vladimir's Seminary Press, 2009), 38.
7. Theokritoff, *Living*, 38.

8. John 1:32.

9. Metropolitan Kallistos Ware, *Through the Creation to the Creator* (Friends of the Centre, 1996).

10. Mark I. Wallace, *When God Was a Bird* (Fordham University Press, 2019), 22.

Chapter 12: On Evil

1. Jeffrey Burton Russell, *The Devil: Perceptions of Evil from Antiquity to Primitive Christianity* (Cornell University Press, 1977), 55.

2. Peter Shaffer, *Equus* (Scribner, 2005).

3. Shaffer, *Equus*, 65.

4. Shaffer, *Equus*, 103.

5. Shaffer, *Equus*, 81.

6. Shaffer, *Equus*, 83.

7. Jeffrey Burton Russell, *The Devil: Perceptions of Evil from Antiquity to Primitive Christianity* (Cornell University Press, 1977).

8. Russell, *The Devil.*

9. Richard Beck, *Reviving Old Scratch* (Fortress Press, 2016).

10. Acts 10:38.

11. Mark 1:32–34.

12. Richard Beck, *Reviving Old Scratch* (Fortress Press, 2016), 104.

13. Bayard Rustin, quoted on bronze plaque, 340 West 28th Street, New York City, his residence from 1962 to 1987.

14. Keith Thomas, *Religion and the Decline of Magic: Studies in Popular Beliefs in Sixteenth and Seventeenth Century England* (Weidenfeld and Nicolson, 1971), 498.

15. Sir Thomas More, quoted in Keith Thomas, *Religion and the Decline of Magic: Studies in Popular Beliefs in Sixteenth and Seventeenth Century England* (Weidenfeld and Nicolson, 1971).

16. Robert Burton, quoted in Keith Thomas, *Religion and the Decline of Magic: Studies in Popular Beliefs in Sixteenth and Seventeenth Century England* (Weidenfeld and Nicolson, 1971), 275.

17. Keith Thomas, *Religion and the Decline of Magic: Studies in Popular Beliefs*

in Sixteenth and Seventeenth Century England (Weidenfeld and Nicolson, 1971), 275.

18. Richard Gilbert, quoted in Keith Thomas, *Religion and the Decline of Magic: Studies in Popular Beliefs in Sixteenth and Seventeenth Century England* (Weidenfeld and Nicolson, 1971), 201.

Chapter 13: On Praise Making

1. Jalal al-Din Rumi, *Open Secret: Versions of Rumi,* trans. Coleman Barks and John Moyne (Threshold Books, 1984), 51.
2. John Keats, letter to his brothers (Dec. 1817).

Epilogue: On the Ancient Good

1. Elizabeth Rees, *Celtic Saints: Passionate Wanderers* (Thames & Hudson Ltd., 2000).
2. John Moriarty, *A Hut at the Edge of the Village*, ed. Martin Shaw (Lilliput Press, 2021).
3. Wallace Black Elk, in conversation with the author, spring 1997.

Index